INNER SKIING

REVISED EDITION

INNER

W. TIMOTHY GALLWEY

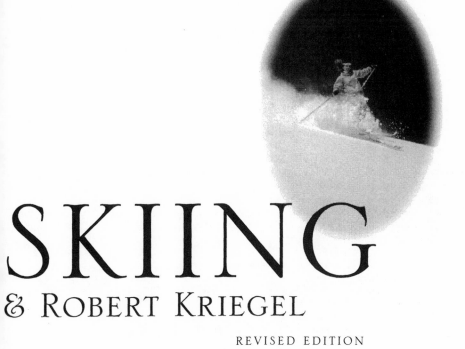

SKIING

& ROBERT KRIEGEL

REVISED EDITION

RANDOM HOUSE   NEW YORK

This is a revised edition of *Inner Skiing*, published by Random House in 1977.

Grateful acknowledgment is made to the following for permission to reprint previously published material:
Macmillan Publishing Co., Inc., and Turnstone Press, Ltd., London: Excerpts from *Jonathan Livingston Seagull* by Richard Bach. Copyright © 1970 by Richard D. Bach. Reprinted by permission.
California Living, The Magazine of the San Francisco Sunday Examiner & Chronicle: Excerpts from "California Living." Copyright © 1977 by *California Living,* The Magazine of the San Francisco Sunday Examiner & Chronicle. Reprinted by permission.

Library of Congress Cataloging-in-Publication Data
Gallwey, W. Timothy.
    Inner skiing/W. Timothy Gallwey and Robert Kriegel.—Rev. ed.
      p.   cm.
    ISBN 0-679-77827-6
    1. Skis and skiing—Psychological aspects.   I. Kriegel, Robert.
  II. Title.
  GV854.9.P75G34 1997
  796.93'01'9—dc21   97-20805

Random House website address: http://www.randomhouse.com/
Printed in the United States of America on acid-free paper

Book design by Lilly Langotsky
BVG 01

To Maharaji
with greatest respect
and gratitude
TG

With great love
to the memory of my
father, Arthur Kriegel
RK

Desire is like a force. One force is generated by our thoughts, and one is generated naturally within our hearts, and just where these forces are directed determines how useful or harmful they are.

Maharaji

FOREWORD: THE FIRE AND THE FORM

Since the publication of *The Inner Game of Tennis* in 1974, it has been most interesting to observe the radical changes in how skiing is taught. I was surprised to find that many professional ski instructors were eagerly exploring the ideas presented in that book, even more than were most tennis instructors. Well before I decided to coauthor *Inner Skiing* with Bob Kriegel, ski instructors at Vail and Aspen were actively applying the Inner Game principles and techniques to the teaching of skiing.

Although I did not know it at the time, this interest was due in no small measure to the groundwork and pedagogical leadership of Austrian-born Horst Abraham. Abraham was the director of education and development at the Vail Ski School and served in the same capacity for the national organization of ski instructors (PSIA) for thirteen years. Educated in Vienna, he had earned the highest certification status in Austria, France, and Germany as a ski instructor, but early in his career he began to openly question the validity of the authoritarian Austrian teaching style. He finally left the country, pressured by the Austrian ski gurus who felt challenged by his desire to innovate. Coming to America, he found a supportive reception in Aspen and later in Vail, where he combined broad knowledge of ski techniques with the ideas of psychologists Carl Rogers, Abraham Maslow, and other educational thinkers. Gradually, the ski world saw a refreshing shift away from rigid uniformity and toward teaching and learning methods designed to explore and facilitate the natural learning process.

So in the mid-seventies when Abraham invited me to address the assembled body of ski instructors at Vail Mountain about the Inner Game, I was surprised to find over two hundred instructors assembled. I started my talk by trying to explain how the principle of nonjudgmental awareness applied to the teaching of skiing. Within a few minutes, I noticed that although the instructors seemed to be listening, they were sitting in rather defensive positions in their chairs. Guessing the reason, I immediately changed directions. Dropping all references to skiing, I shifted the focus to an account of what I had learned about the natural learning process while teaching *tennis*. Immediately the defenses dropped. The instructors shifted forward in their chairs and hung on every word, laughing and clearly making connections with their own experience. When I finished, they expressed their appreciation with a standing ovation.

Afterward, instructor after instructor came up to talk with me and in effect said the same thing: "You know, Tim, it's the same in skiing!" "Really?" I would say, feigning surprise. "In what ways is it the same?" With professional competitiveness out of the way, the instructors were willing to openly discuss their observations about the efficacy of simple awareness of edges and skis, turns, or even gravity. They also related anecdotes of how that self-critical, overcontrolling voice I called Self 1 was as much of a hindrance on the ski slopes as on the tennis courts.

As in tennis, the skier was at his or her best only when the mind was quiet and focused. Then skiers experienced the spontaneous excellence that was characteristic of Self 2 in all sports. It became obvious that instructors and students alike needed to become adept at quieting their judgmental, overly analytical Self 1 in order to gain access to the innate and magical competencies of their Self 2.

Ideas like these might have been considered too far out at that time if Abraham had not paved the way for them. Fortunately, he and his colleagues on the Education Committee knew enough to assemble specialists in the field of biomechanics, education, kinesiology, and psychology so it would be difficult to easily dismiss such new thinking and practice. As ski instructors experimented with this more student- and learning-centered approach, many found that they could help skiers avoid much of the frustration and awkwardness previously thought to be a normal part of learning to ski. When the traditional request to conform to "proper form" was replaced with an open invitation to explore possibilities, students became more in touch with their bodies. As a result, their inherent natural learning abilities had a better chance to emerge.

Soon there was an energetic, ongoing conversation in the skiing community about fundamental principles and techniques of teaching core skiing skills. One of the reasons ski instructors could move ahead of the coaches of other sports in understanding the learning process was that they had regular interaction with one another. Unlike the pros at golf and tennis clubs, most ski instructors are part of ski schools that often comprise hundreds of instructors who meet together, teach on the same mountain, and have daily occasion to discuss and debate learning and teaching ideas. Moreover, the methodology used by any particular ski school could add or detract from the school's reputation and thus become a significant factor influencing the profitability of the resort. Revenues reflect the number of new beginners attracted as well as the retention of repeat students. Therefore, each school wanted to be known as having the most advanced and user-friendly methods of instruction.

Yet it was because of the intellectual leadership of people like Horst Abraham, a true educator, that the conversation reached higher degrees of sophistication. Through his leadership, a new approach to ski instruction called the American Teaching Method emerged. ATM combined an understanding of the human learning process with new observations about effective technique in a way that was very distinct from earlier Austrian dogma. It presented the international ski world with an alternative to the European domination of ski teaching and brought with it a greater focus on the student.

Around the same time, *Inner Skiing* emerged on the scene and became popular enough among skiers to make *The New York Times Book Review*'s nonfiction best-seller list. The book showed how skiing could be learned directly from experience. There were two keys to learning from experience. The first involved a heightened, *nonjudgmental awareness* in the moment. This awareness was gained by paying ever-increasing attention to what happens in different parts of the body, as well as to the precise action of the skis on the given terrain. The second key was the simple *trust* in one's potential gained directly from experience. The skiers who learned how to trust themselves improved their performance without having to rely on a menu of "do's and don'ts" issued by instructors to make *your* body move in conformity with *their* current model of "good skiing." In order to achieve desired levels of awareness and trust, it was necessary, the book put forth, to quiet the critical and overcontrolling voices in the mind.

Not surprisingly, the response from ski instructors to these principles was mixed. A lively debate ensued around such ideas as nonjudgmental body and ski awareness, playful learning, imagery, learning from experience, exploration, engaging in the magic of rhythmic movement, dealing with fear, facilitating learning rather than teaching, and exploring domains of skills rather than teaching rigid technique. Those who had firsthand experience of the natural learning phenomena discovered that the principles were valid and found methods of instruction that took a great deal of pressure off both instructor and student. Skiers and many instructors felt less constrained and were able to explore the expression of their own bodies and unique personalities through their skiing and teaching. It not only made learning to ski easier and more fun, but for many it allowed skiing to become a metaphor for the freedom and autonomy that they wanted to bring into the rest of their lives.

At the same time, there was defensiveness on the part of those instructors who were not ready to let go of teaching standardized skiing technique. Of course, this position found valid support from the obvious fact that technical knowledge of skiing *can* be an asset in the learning process. The debate became somewhat polarized between ATM, which used technique as background knowledge and favored the simplicity of the inner skiing approach, and those who wanted to teach technique alone. The latter group relied on curriculum-focused teaching and were a force pulling the pendulum toward formalism and teacher dependency. Not surprisingly, some students wanted instructors who would yell the "do's and don'ts" at them. After all, that's what most of us have been conditioned to think we are paying for! Many instructors felt it difficult to find an appropriate balance between what they saw as a "soft" humanistic approach to learning and the "hard" technical disciplines.

The original version of *Inner Skiing* was clearly on the natural-learning side of this debate primarily because its true advantages had not been adequately represented. Even now, I find little that I would want to change in the original text. The principles and techniques are as valid now as they ever were. Principles such as body awareness, trusting natural instincts, learning by paying attention, and the simple enjoyment of skiing no longer seem new to most. And it is now common understanding that there is a big difference between knowing something in the head and knowing it in one's body. Yet overinstruction on the part of instructors and overcontrol on the part of the skier still get in the way of spontaneous excellence on the slopes.

One of the instructional myths that prevailed in skiing as well as tennis and golf was that one should imitate the pros. If you want to learn how to swing or turn correctly, observe the best as they swing or turn and then do likewise. The observation of pros at their best was made easier by advances in video camera technology that could slow rapid movements so they could be analyzed and described in detail. Using the same technology, skiers, with the help of their instructors, could analyze where their technique differed from that of the pros. Then they could go back to the slopes and try to make the appropriate changes.

Of course the mistake in this kind of thinking is that what is right for the pro may not be right for the recreational skier. Even though an acorn has the potential to become an oak, it doesn't mean that it can reach that potential by imitating the full-grown tree. For example, racers who are recorded at high speeds will make moves that no skier could make at slower speeds without falling over.

Realizing that the new teaching philosophy was leaving most skiers and many instructors somewhat bewildered, Abraham and his team added structure to the system by emphasizing universal core skills such as dynamic balance, pressure control, edging, and rotary movements. These core skills were meant to become the "playing field" for both learners and instructors to allow for exploration and discovery of an integrated development of skills. This approach added a simplicity and spirit of innovation that brought new life to learning the sport and, after a few years, gained international respect.

Later, after the broad acceptance of this approach, the spirit of discovery that had given it birth began to fade. Instructors focused on the new structural elements of the method as if they were final forms, and rigidity started to set in again. Milton Beens, the current education director of the PSIA, and one of the originators of Centerline, pointed out to me recently that as soon as any method becomes accepted and instructors are required to teach it to be certified, the underlying strength of the method tends to be replaced by rote learning and dogmatism without true understanding. Living in a culture that is very results-oriented, it is easy for part-time ski instructors to settle for teaching whatever they are told to teach instead of making the effort to think for themselves and to understand the dynamics of learning itself.

So the pendulum swings in small and wide arcs between the *fire* of spontaneous learning and the *form* of dogmatism of one kind or another. Not being a student of skiing technique itself, I have never been interested in the debates about which "outer" technique is better than another. *Inner Skiing* is about how best to learn whatever technique you decide you want to learn. Chapter 7, "Discovering Skiing Technique," is a new chapter that puts forth a simple way of bridging the gap between the methodology of natural learning and that of technical instruction without bias as to the school of instruction. The focus is on learning how to learn and how to get out of your own way. This chapter will offer a way of using technical knowledge to facilitate natural learning without the crippling judgments, doubts, and other obstacles that normally attend it.

In addition to the growth of instructional understanding, the ski world has seen a continuous development in skiing equipment. This has had significant impact on the process of learning to ski and caused changes in technique itself. As in tennis and golf, the use of new materials and the changes in size and shape of the equipment have required of recreational and professional skiers alike a continuous willingness to learn and to adapt to change. From my point of view, this is a welcome influence. Anything that prompts us to adapt, change, and keep learning not only moves us to overcome our human tendency to get stuck in rigid patterns, but also prepares us for the kind of learning that is now a necessity in a rapidly changing world.

I find it fascinating and even somewhat amusing to note that just when the pendulum in skiing doctrine was swinging again to the "rigid" side, snowboarding landed on the slopes with an unceremonious but loud exclamation: "We're *here!* And we're not interested in *any* doctrine. We are inventing a totally new way of moving ourselves over the snow and through the air above the snow." Of course at first this voice came from the young, the brave, and the restless, intent on pushing not only the limits of their freedom, but sometimes the boundaries of safety as well. Early on, there were no formal instructors of the sport. Snowboarding was being invented by those who wanted to break out of every mold by exploring new possibilities and avoiding conformity to old ones. New moves and more radical tricks, as well as a whole new language to describe and praise them, were being designed every day. At the same time boots, bindings, and boards were being tweaked and fixed by the innovative boarders who were using them. The snowboarder had no choice but to learn from experience. The spirit of this developing sport has been contagious and the pace of its innovation "gnarly" to say the least. It is helping to push the pendulum, stuck for a time in the realm of formalism, back again toward the fire of freedom.

For better or worse, the first stage of the sport has passed. People over thirty can be seen carving turns on boards now made by sophisticated manufacturers. Glossy magazines are advertising snowboarding equipment; books of instruction are appearing, and snowboarding instructors are available at most ski resorts. And of course national and international associations have emerged that want to regulate and hopefully preserve the innovative spirit that brought this new and rapidly growing sport into being.

Chapter 9, "Learning to Snowboard," looks at the benefits of learning to snowboard as well as an approach to doing so with relative safety and ease. Perhaps what is most difficult about learning to snowboard is also the most beneficial. I asked Pat McNamara, a fifty-three-year-old competitive snowboarder who teaches many skiers the joys he has found in snowboarding, what was most difficult for skiers in learning to snowboard. He explained that the learning curve in snowboarding was much faster than in skiing but that experienced skiers sometimes found it difficult to become beginners again. "It takes a kind of humility that is not going to resist starting again on the bunny slopes even after being able to ski down black diamond slopes with total control."

The willingness to be a beginner is an essential ingredient to being a good learner—no matter what your level of expertise. It is the willingness to "not know" and to be comfortable with not knowing that makes both children and adults able to learn without fear. For me to do this, I have to drop my image of competence and be willing to start anew. This is the same kind of transition that many skiers may also be facing in their work lives as new technologies and reorganizations require mastering totally new skills. Modern life is not very kind to ruts. Everyone is being required to unlearn old ways of doing things and to be able to adapt to changes without losing balance. We are all being called to rediscover the inherent talent for learning we have as human beings—even if it takes some humility.

So "Learning to Snowboard" is not so much about snowboarding as it is about learning. It is about how and why one might want to consider learning to snowboard. It is about the value of not getting stuck in ruts, and it is about learning how to learn in a way that does not push the envelope of safety to extreme limits. Whether or not the reader is already engaged in snowboarding or has already decided never to put two feet sideways on a single plank, this chapter is an invitation to find your balance between the *fire* of what is spontaneous and new and the *form* that distills the best of what is old.

I have always seen skiing as an expression of the human desire to extend freedom and range of movement. Whether on one or two boards, it will always be thrilling to glide down terrain at speeds many times faster than feet alone allow. To do so with grace, elegance, and courage will never lose its attraction. So above all sports that I know, skiing is one that should never be overprescribed. This is not the sport for practicing conforming to boundaries and doctrines. It is a sport for experiencing one's freedom and trust in one's inner balance. This alone can assure the necessary outer balance while moving at high speed.

Skiing is also a sport where one is vulnerable to the injury of self or others. New equipment that's faster, slicker, and sharper makes it easier to reach speeds beyond one's control. On the wide-open slopes groomed by the modern ski areas, it's easier than ever to not realize how fast you are actually going until you have to stop to avoid someone. Everyone on the slopes needs a heightened awareness of others on the mountain as well as of the limits of his or her own abilities to keep in control. This sport can be a matchless metaphor for modern life, which continuously calls on us to master movement through ever-changing and unexpected terrain while remaining conscious enough to protect the safety of ourselves and others.

I hope that this new edition of *Inner Skiing* will increase your level of enjoyment of this magnificent sport and at the same time bring greater ease and effectiveness to your learning and growth, both on and off the ski slopes.

AUTHOR'S NOTE

The reader of a book written by two people deserves an explanation of how the authors combined their efforts. Though I realized that Inner Game principles had a practical contribution to make to skiing, my background in the sport was limited, and Bob Kriegel had not only the necessary experience in skiing and psychology, but also a practical understanding of the Inner Game. Consequently *Inner Skiing* is truly a collaborative effort; each of us shared in its conception and in the writing. Generally we would tape long discussions on the content and organization of each chapter, and from this Bob would then write a first draft. (For this reason the first person almost always refers to Bob.) I would write the second draft, and then we would polish this together.

The changes in this revised edition, including the Foreword and the chapters "Discovering Skiing Technique" and "Learning to Snowboard," are authored by myself.

—T. G.

ACKNOWLEDGMENTS

With sincere thanks to:

Cathy Modrell, one of the most knowledgeable women in the field of ski instruction and one of my first instructors, whose collaborative efforts on the new edition are especially appreciated;

Hans Rawat, an outstanding young skier and snowboarder who gave generously of his time and common sense to explain to me the attraction of the craft and culture of snowboarding;

Horst Abraham, one of the country's leading ski educators, whose acknowledgment of *Inner Skiing* from its inception to the present has given it a place of respect in the world of skiing—with special appreciation for his perspective and contribution to the new technical chapter of the revised edition;

Leslye Deitch, who is too fond of her footing on the ground to have tried skiing, but whose very groundedness and loyal support have helped me navigate all-too-many self-made moguls;

Pat McNamara, my one and only snowboarding coach, whose belief and passion for the sport have encouraged many besides the young and daring to become advocates without throwing caution to the wind;

Peter Kronig—the grand master of ski instruction from Zermatt, Switzerland, and my ski coach and friend of twenty years—who has inspired and encouraged *Inner Skiing* from the beginning.

CONTENTS

INNER SKIING

REVISED EDITION

1❄

SKIING IS
MORE
THAN A
PARALLEL
TURN

T here is a magic in skiing when all is going well that transcends anything I have experienced in other sports. As I soar down a mountainside letting my body find its own balance in turn after turn, my mind as clear as the cold air against my face, my heart feels as warm as the sun, and I attain a level of experience which compels me to return to the snow for more and more of the same.

But too often this magic turns to misery. Apprehensive thoughts intrude and I lose natural rhythm, repeat old mistakes, and fall needlessly. I pick myself up cold, wet, and discouraged, wondering if skiing is worth the trouble after all. Will I ever get off the seemingly endless plateau in my progress and ski the way I'd like to? Will I ever soar again? Something tells me not to count on it, but another voice urges me to try.

The purpose of *Inner Skiing* is to increase the magic of skiing and decrease the misery—to bypass the frustrations that inhibit its joy and freedom, and to learn how to reach that state of mind in which we not only appreciate the sport but perform at our best. The premise of this approach is that primarily it is neither external conditions nor lack of technical expertise that prevents us from experiencing skiing at its best, but the doubts, fears, and thoughts within our own heads. The Inner Skier comes to recognize that his greatest challenge, and consequently his greatest possibilities, lies in overcoming the self-imposed mental limitations that prevent the full expression of his physical potential.

The fears and doubts in the mind are automatically transferred to the body in the form of tension, rigidity, and awkwardness, preventing us not only from moving fluidly, but also from seeing the terrain clearly. Inner Skiing aims to develop the skills necessary to recognize and overcome these inner obstacles. Using this approach, the skier learns the art of relaxed concentration and to trust his body's potential to learn and perform. He discovers that the secret to success in skiing lies in not trying too hard, and that his best teacher is his own experience. He develops a true sense of self-confidence that allows him to view falls and mistakes as learning opportunities rather than reasons for anger and frustration.

The Inner Game approach is hardly new. It is similar to the natural way that, as children, we learned to walk, talk, or throw a ball. It uses the unconscious, rather than the deliberately self-conscious, mind. This process doesn't have to be learned; we already know it. All that is needed is to unlearn the habits and concepts that interfere with our natural learning ability, and to trust the innate intelligence of our bodies.

The principles of the Inner Game approach to learning and to maximum performance are basically the same for most sports and other activities, but each sport presents its own unique inner and outer challenges. Tennis requires sustained visual concentration during long periods of physical exertion. Distance running offers special opportunities to overcome boredom and develop endurance. Golf demands the subtlest kind of mental concentration and kinesthetic control. Team sports teach us cooperation and how to sacrifice individual egos for the benefit of the team. The remainder of this chapter concerns the often-neglected opportunities offered by the special nature of skiing to learn some things more universally applicable than how to make a parallel turn. The parallel turn is not difficult once we rediscover *how* to learn.

LETTING GO OF WHAT YOU THINK YOU KNOW

Remember how strange and awkward it felt the first time you stepped into ski boots and strapped those long boards onto your feet? Remember how frightened and out of control you felt when you tried to move?

Most sports have one characteristic in common. Whether it is baseball, basketball, tennis, golf, hiking, climbing, or boxing, the way we move on the earth is by walking or running. Even as beginners ignorant of the rudiments of these sports, we at least know how to move. But in skiing we must slide rather than walk or run, and so we relate to the ground and move on it in an entirely different way. When we first stand on a pair of skis we lose that feeling of having a firm foothold on solid ground. A slight shift of weight can cause us to lose our balance and fall.

Thus, in skiing we must confront a basic fear: *loss of the familiar.*

This feeling of uncertainty is similar to the first time we put our feet on the pedals of a bicycle, pushed off the wall of an ice-skating rink or tried to stay afloat in water. Just as in these other activities, learning to ski requires first being willing to let go of one known sense of control in order to gain another. In trying to do so, few of us escape a sense of panic. Learning to swim, we flail around in the water desperately trying to stay afloat. In skiing we hold our bodies rigid, hoping to prevent ourselves from falling. But our struggle to maintain control in a new medium usually interferes with more than it helps the effort to achieve that goal. Fighting the new element prevents us from adapting to it.

Our situation as a beginning skier is similar to being in a room when the lights go out. In pitch-blackness our eyes—the primary means for gathering information about our world—are useless; we are literally in the dark. If we panic and grope blindly for the light, inevitably we will bump into objects and damage them or ourselves. On the other hand, if we allow our eyes to adjust to the dark, shapes will start to emerge and we will again feel secure. Similarly, in trying to ski, if we don't panic and fight the experience of sliding, our bodies soon grow accustomed to this new form of locomotion and we gain a sense of confidence.

Not having his basic references for moving his body, the frightened beginning skier tries to cling to his old and familiar ways. When trying to slow down or stop, his first reaction is to lean back and dig in his heels, just as he would when walking or running. In trying to prevent himself from falling down, he leans uphill. But in skiing, the laws of movement are different, and leaning back only makes you go faster, while leaning uphill causes the skis to slide out from under you. To the beginner, this reaction of his skis is as confusing as if he had stepped on the brakes of his car, only to find it accelerating. He panics even more and leans back still further in a desperate attempt to stop, which causes him to increase speed, lose balance, and fall.

I will always remember my first time on skis. I rode a rope tow to the top of a small hill, positioned myself in a basic snowplow as I had seen other beginners do, and pushed off. As soon as I began moving I became petrified at not knowing how to stop or slow down. My body, bent almost in half, was stiff with fear; I felt that if I relaxed one tightened muscle I would crash to the ground. In effect, I was a sliding statue. At first, whenever I began going too fast or reached the bottom, I would fall backward, the only way I knew to stop. After a few runs, when I began to descend less slowly, the falls became more spectacular. Looking for a less painful way to stop, I tried unsuccessfully to stab my poles into the snow in front of me. My frustration only made me more determined to try still harder, biting my tongue and tensing my jaw. But the more I tried, the tighter I became, and the more I fell.

Finally I said to myself, The hell with it. I'm going to stop fighting the hill and just ski. If I fall, I fall. I can't do any worse than I'm doing now. With this I felt a little more relaxed, and though it was scary to just let myself slide down, and though I still felt out of control, I didn't fall as frequently. After a few more runs, I started feeling my skis and noticing what happened when I leaned to one side or the other, or backward and forward. Gradually, by going with this new sliding motion, I began to gain a little control. Though I knew I wasn't turning properly, I was soon able to get where I wanted and to stop without falling. I was going to learn to ski after all!

Like anything else, learning to ski is a process of discovery that comes primarily from the experience itself. As we let go of our preconceived notions about how to move, we feel what it is like to slide on the snow. Without straining, our body learns from its experience, just as it did when learning to swim or ride a bike. By not resisting this new experience as we negotiate a slope we can learn far more than simply a new form of locomotion; we learn how to deal with the unexpected wherever we encounter it. We discover that we can adapt to strange or different experiences only when we are willing to let go of our dependence on old concepts.

A CHANCE TO OVERCOME FEAR

As he improves, the skier naturally wants to ski faster and take more difficult runs, to leave the slopes on which he is comfortable and try something new. But while taking his first chair to the top of the mountain or attempting a harder trail is exciting, it is also frightening.

Exceeding previous limits always involves risk and usually some fear, but it is the natural growth process that started when we first left the comfort and safety of the womb. The first time we attempt a more difficult slope, we take a chance on losing control; we may fall and get hurt or fail and be humiliated. Risk is like a pendulum: at one end of the swing is the excitement of growth and discovery; at the other end is fear.

Fear, which is probably the biggest obstacle to any learning process, is a repressive force. It exists in the mind, and almost always it is based on something that *might* happen in the future, rather than what *is* happening now. As Don Juan, the Yaqui Indian sorcerer, says, it is "the first of man's natural enemies . . . a terrible enemy, treacherous and difficult to overcome . . . If the man terrified in its presence runs away, his enemy will have put an end to his quest . . . he will never learn."

Learning to confront and overcome fear is one of the biggest challenges and opportunities in skiing. But it is not easy; in fact, it is often more difficult to overcome fear than to actually ski the slope itself. Yet as Don Juan says, "He must not run away, he must defy his fear . . . and take the next step in learning . . . and a moment will come when this enemy will retreat."

8

A skier may resist this challenge, saying, "I just want to learn to ski, not to overcome fear." But fear will slow his learning, and if and when he does improve despite remaining fearful, the skills he has mastered will be limited to the slopes. The Inner Skier chooses to confront and overcome fear. As a result, he improves not only his skiing, but also the quality of his life. Chapter 4, "Fear of Falling, Failing, and Flying," will treat this subject more comprehensively.

COOPER-ATING WITH NATURE

Watch an expert skier descend a trail: he flows like water in a mountain stream. He shifts weight to one side, then another, producing a series of smooth looping turns. By the slightest move of his legs his direction changes. It seems so simple and natural; in contrast to the beginner's movements his seem effortless.

Skiing is similar to riding a bicycle downhill. Both acts require less physical and mental effort than we imagine. On a bike we need only sit, hold the handlebars, and let the hill take us. As we pick up speed the bike responds to subtle movements of our hands with nearly no effort on our part. We lean slightly into each turn; balance is maintained without conscious thought, and the power is supplied by gravity. Skiing, too, can be effortless when we cooperate with gravity's forces instead of fighting them.

In most sports we rely on our own power to run or jump, throw a ball, or swing a racket. But in skiing, gravity provides the power and pulls us down the slope. The only exertion necessary is to play with the pull—checking, turning, slowing, and directing our movement.

Learning to play with this natural force is a useful experience in everyday living. From it we can learn to act in harmony with our changing surroundings, other people, and ourselves. Relying on gravity clearly demonstrates the advantages of blending with and using existing forces to move toward a chosen goal.

During an off-mountain session of an Inner Skiing workshop I asked for two volunteers of about the same size. Keith, a young, bearded psychologist, and Arnie, a rugged-looking real estate entrepreneur in his forties, came forward. "Stand facing each other and hold your hands out shoulder height so that you are touching palms," I instructed. "Now the goal of this exercise is to get the other person off balance. You can move your hands any way you want. The only rule is that you can't move your feet, and that your hands must keep touching the other person's with the palms open. Okay, begin."

All became quiet as Keith and Arnie started moving their hands in big circles, giving a push here, a feint there. Then Arnie gave a hard shove forward, almost knocking Keith over backward. Recovering, Keith also started pushing in earnest. For the next few minutes the only sounds were the grunts of the two participants as they strained for an advantage.

Suddenly it seemed as if Keith was winning. Using his superior strength, he was slowly pushing Arnie's arms backward. All looked lost for Arnie, until abruptly he relaxed his arms, causing Keith to lurch forward.

"Perfect," I said as everybody clapped and the two men sat down. "When Keith and Arnie tried to resist each other's strength, they used a lot of energy and tired quickly. But eventually Arnie won by blending with Keith's force and using it to his advantage. Blending, a basic principle in the martial arts, can also be used in skiing, teaching us when to flow with the force of gravity and when to resist it."

Later that morning I could feel fear in the air as a group of us stood at the top of a steep, moguled slope. "Maybe we should try another slope," Kerry said hesitantly. "This looks like crash city." A few others agreed.

"Let's try looking at the bumps in a different way," I suggested, trying to ease the tension. "Look at the slope as if it were an opponent in the 'push hands' game. Let's try to *use* the moguls to help us turn, instead of fighting against them the way most of us usually do."

The others in the group were hesitant, but Diane, who had been quite silent all week, suddenly came alive. "We can even thank them for helping us," she suggested.

"Fine," said Keith. "Let's thank every mogul we use," and he started off. Everybody followed, and it was comical to hear eight skiers going down this difficult slope yelling out "Thank you." Everyone seemed more relaxed and skied better, and those who fell didn't seem to mind. At the bottom, they all were laughing and wanted to do it again. Befriending our enemy had been fun and also had done much to improve our skiing.

Situation Skiing

Skiing is a sport of changes; no two runs are ever the same. Snow that is soft and smooth in the morning becomes rutted and packed down later in the day. Moguls increase in size as skiers keep pushing snow into them. The texture of the surface itself changes with shifts in temperature or exposure to the sun.

"Skiing is a sport of diversity, of differences," says Jean-Claude Killy, the Olympic triple gold medal winner. "To get more out of the mountain and from ourselves, it is important to learn to adjust to these different situations." In powder we sit back slightly on the tails of our skis, whereas if we did this on hardpack we would lose balance.

Many times I have skied a slope that I had taken only a few hours before. Thinking that I know it well enough, I will take it for granted and let my mind wander, when suddenly I'll hit the unexpected—a patch of ice, a bare spot or a new mogul—and be thrown off balance, lose my rhythm, perhaps even fall. When you have preconceived notions about a slope, you won't truly experience it. You see the slope as you think it is, or as it was before, rather than as it is now. When you hit something, it comes as a surprise. This is the mountain's way of saying "Pay attention."

With an awareness that each run is different, we tend to concentrate more. Taking less for granted, we are more alert, our feeling for our skis and the snow increases, and our sensitivity to any changes in the terrain heightens. When the mind is in this state of alertness, the body is poised and ready to respond to any situation. Not only does our skiing improve, but we also have more fun.

The more we realize that nothing in this world ever stays the same, and that change is the only constant, the more acute our perceptions will be. We begin to see the world as it is, rather than through the screen of past concepts. The present seems alive and fresh, and we are more able to respond appropriately to the novelty and difference inherent in each moment.

SLOWING DOWN TO SEE

When I lived in New York City, I remember longing to spend a few days in the country away from the cement, fumes, and frantic rush. I'd dream about walking through the woods, feeling the earth under my feet, seeing the sky overhead. Then I'd get away for a weekend and be in such a hurry I'd never even notice where I was.

What was I doing on these trips? Frantic skiing, of course. My friends and I would leave the city on Friday evening, drive for five hours and arrive exhausted. Nevertheless, we'd awaken at dawn, gulp down breakfast, and rush to the mountain, where we'd ski all day, not stopping even for lunch. The only chance we had to relax was in the lift lines, but of course we were tense there as well, moaning about how slowly the lines were moving. Whenever the chair stopped, the delay was like death.

For all the nature I took in on those weekends, I might as well have been skiing in the Manhattan subway. Sure, I'd be looking out at my surroundings, but mostly to gauge how long the lift line was going to be, or on which slope the snow was best.

Then one Saturday I was coming alone down a big bowl, only to find, after thirty yards, that it was crusty and unskiable. I was too far down to return to the top, so I had to cross over and hike uphill to reach an adjoining slope. I was really annoyed; precious skiing time was being wasted. When I reached the top of the slope, I was out of breath and stopped to rest. At this moment the light on a patch of snow caught my eye. It looked as if the snow was bursting with all the colors of the spectrum. Suddenly it occurred to me that in all my years of skiing in some of the most beautiful places in the world, I had never really opened my eyes. I looked around, seeing as if for the first time the colors of the trees, the snow, the sky, and the shapes of the mountains on the horizon.

That evening, still moved by this encounter with nature, I decided to stay in our lodge rather than go partying with my friends. Watching the fire dance in the hearth, I realized that the way I had been skiing was a reflection of my life. Everything was done in a rush; I worked, came home, changed clothes, and went out again. I thought I had to move fast or I'd be left behind.

Seeing that light reflecting off the snow changed my approach and attitude not just to skiing, but to life in general. Today I would rather take my time feeling the exhilaration of my body in motion, and observing the beauty of my surroundings, than rush down the mountain in order to get in a few more runs. I also see the futility of thinking that more is necessarily better, whether in ski runs or possessions. I have begun to pay more attention to the quality of what I am doing rather than to the quantity.

TO WIN IS TO ENJOY

When we participate in a sport in which the object is winning or reaching a destination point, we tend to think about the score, the goal, the end of the journey. Our efforts are concentrated on what we must do to beat our opponent, and if we aren't winning, we aren't enjoying. But the pleasures of skiing lie in being totally involved, in the way we feel when the body is in motion—the delight in a turn skillfully executed, the sense of our own natural rhythm and flow. The goal is a feeling of harmony both with ourselves and with our environment. The prize is in the process itself. Hence, skiing can teach us something that is often overlooked in our goal-oriented daily activities: *the importance of enjoying the process.* From it we can learn that without appreciating the path, reaching the goal is often meaningless. Moreover, we discover that games of all kinds are more often won when first they are enjoyed.

So there *is* more to skiing than learning parallel turns. For the skier who recognizes the further possibilities his sport offers for learning how to learn, for overcoming fears and self-doubt, for gaining concentration and appreciation for nature, skiing becomes *re-creation* in the original sense of the word: an opportunity to discover something important about oneself and to learn skills that improve not only one's skiing but the quality of one's life.

2 ❄
SELF 1 AND
SELF 2

All of us have had those incredible runs when for some reason everything seems to click and we ski so much better than usual that we surprise ourselves. Turns we've been struggling with are suddenly easy. Frustrations vanish and we become totally absorbed in the joy of the moment. The usual mental struggle—trying to do everything right, worrying about how we look or about falling and failing—is forgotten. Enjoyment is so intense that we don't even think of making a mistake—and we don't. The thinking mind is in a state of rest; awareness is at a peak. For a time, self-imposed limitations are forgotten; we are skiing unconsciously.

Runs like these make us forget tight boots, cold hands, long lift lines, and the eternal dissatisfaction of not skiing as well as we want to. It is the memory of these magical moments that draws us back to the slopes time and again in hopes of recapturing them.

Jan, a twenty-two-year-old college student who had told me that she thought she was too uncoordinated to learn to ski, had just such an experience the fourth day she was on skis.

"It was the first time I took a run and really felt in control," she said. "Up to that point, I was always hesitant, holding back and scared to death. I usually felt so awkward that I didn't believe I could ever learn to make a proper turn. But all my doubts left me on that run. For the first time I felt loose and relaxed, and for some reason it was easy to stop and turn wherever I wanted. I couldn't believe it; I wasn't even afraid of falling. After that one run I felt like a skier!"

"How did that happen?" I asked.

BREAK-THROUGH RUNS

"That's the funny thing, I can't tell you what I did—in fact, I don't think I *did* anything! It just seemed to happen, and I went with it. I felt so free and light!" Jan was obviously still enraptured by the memory of that moment.

I once had a similar experience. I had skied hard all day, but not very well. This was to be my last run, and I resolved to take it easy on a slope that was challenging but not too difficult. But instead of pushing off right away as I usually did, I stood at the top of the run for a moment, taking in the silence of the world around me. Then, as I started down and took a few turns, I knew that something was different. I felt as if I were gliding effortlessly. Instead of planning where to turn, I seemed to know instinctively. I didn't have to think at all; it was as if the mountain was showing me the way. Moguls, usually my enemies, now seemed like old friends. I was turning on them and jumping off them as if I had been doing it all my life. It was more like flying down the mountain! I couldn't believe that I could ski like this.

Halfway down the trail I noticed another skier ahead of me, and I fell in about twenty yards behind him, following his tracks. The two of us floated down the mountain in unison in a silent dance. By the time we reached the bottom I was glowing, and I coasted over to the other skier, whose grin was even bigger than mine. The expression on his face was matched by the exhilaration in his voice as he said, "It was a breakthrough run—my God, I never thought I could ski like that."

Toasting our great run at the bar, my new friend, a surgeon from New York, tried to analyze how without really trying he had skied far better than he ever had before. "You know," he told me, "sometimes I get that same feeling when I'm doing surgery—that sense of total involvement with a greater kind of knowing, and along with it an incredible dexterity and alertness."

This breakthrough experience is one we've all had at different times in our lives. It is the feeling of "getting hot" in a basketball game, of playing "out of your head" in a tennis match, of losing yourself while jogging or swimming. It is the feeling of dancing to music when it seems to be emanating from inside your body. But breakthroughs are not limited to physical activities; they can occur at any time and in any activity. They are those creative flashes when the solution to a problem emerges at the instant you least expect it, the intuitive eureka.

However, much to our chagrin, breakthroughs in skiing or in any other activity virtually never happen when we plan them, and therefore they usually seem accidental. But they don't happen by chance. On the mountain they occur when we are so engrossed that we are no longer thinking about the next turn or judging the last one. In fact, breakthroughs appear *only when we stop thinking.*

This nonthinking, spontaneous state in which we let ourselves float in the experience of the moment is what we call "skiing out of your mind." But like being in love, as soon as we start thinking about how to keep ourselves in this ecstatic state, we lose it. Methodically we then set out to regain our lost sense of mastery by working on our technique, item by item. But the thrill is gone; we are back *in* the mind.

These breakthrough runs, which skiers at all levels experience, have a special significance; they help us to recognize our inherent possibilities. Without them a skier might reasonably conclude that he or she is *innately* awkward or uncoordinated. But the breakthrough confronts us with an undeniable and somewhat uncomfortable truth: we *can* perform much better than we usually do. In light of this realization, our usual excuses—we haven't skied enough recently, haven't had enough lessons, or are just plain uncoordinated—crumble. We can only conclude that the reason we don't normally perform so well is not that we don't have the ability, but that we somehow interfere with it. In the breakthrough run we skied beyond our expectations not because we finally mastered a new technique but because for a few moments our state of mind changed. The mind became quiet, making our movements more natural and coordinated. Such occasions indicate that the excellence of our skiing is dependent more on our state of mind than on the self-conscious mastery of memorized techniques.

To suppress the uncomfortable fact that it is we ourselves who interfere with our ability to ski up to our demonstrated potential, we often prefer to attribute breakthroughs to luck, good snow conditions, newly sharpened edges, or, most commonly, to a tip from another skier. But at some level we understand that in spite of its infrequent occurrence, skiing "out of one's mind" is as natural as running or laughing, that it is a true expression of how skiing could be more often.

I used to spend a lot of time with someone who had these experiences much more than I did. His name was Otis. He was supple and loose; he moved with a natural ease, reacting spontaneously to whatever the situation demanded of him on or off the mountain. His fun-loving attitude was contagious. Without pushing himself or ever trying too hard, Otis was constantly exploring, testing, and going beyond his limits. He seemed to have an inexhaustible supply of energy and complete trust in his body. He was a natural athlete but not at all an uncommon one for his age. He was my first son at the age of four.

I still observe with wonder the joy, excitement, and natural ease of children as they run, jump, climb, and ride their tricycles. I have learned from them how easily and effortlessly we can move when we trust our bodies to do what they know best. As children we were all natural athletes; each of us had that sense of ease and excitement as we rejoiced in the movement of our bodies. The games lasted past dark, ending only with a parent's repeated yells to come in for dinner. There were endless days of excitement, of laughing and crying, of dirty knees, ripped shirts, and scraped elbows. It was a time when everybody played unselfconsciously, a time so filled with breakthrough moments that we were oblivious to them.

Carrie Bachelder, an instructor in our Inner Skiing clinic, told me about playing a children's game with her class. "I was the hare and they were all hounds chasing after me, yelling and growling, trying to catch me. They totally forgot all about do's and don'ts. At the bottom of the run, Terry, a college professor, said, 'I felt like a kid again. I was so intent on catching the hare that I forgot all about my skiing, and, you know, I think I skied better than I have all week. I haven't had fun like that in years.' The other 'hounds' reported similar improvement."

In their preoccupation with the chase, Terry and the others were allowing themselves to ski without thinking. As a result, they recaptured the spontaneous quality of physical play they had known as children, and rediscovered a state of mind conducive to peak performance.

BREAK-THROUGH TO BREAK-DOWN

The morning after our breakthrough run, I met my friend the surgeon again. In fact, we almost crashed into each other; he was careening off a mogul, limbs flying in all directions. After what seemed like an eternity in this position, he fell and passed me in a slide that would have made the late Jackie Robinson envious. Muttering to himself through clenched teeth, he got up slowly, beating the snow with his ski pole as if it were to blame for his crash landing.

Gradually Doc calmed down and we took a few runs together. But he certainly was skiing less well than he had the day before. His movements, which had been so natural and easy, were now stiff and forced, and he was hesitant and visibly frustrated. If the day before had produced a breakthrough, today was a breakdown.

Later, back at the lodge, Doc said "I just don't understand how on one run I can do everything right, and then fall apart on the next."

Then in the next breath Doc proceeded to explain exactly why this happened. That morning he had been so eager to try to repeat yesterday's experience that as he started down he began giving himself helpful suggestions: "Remember, keep your weight forward . . . Edge a little more . . . Don't forget to step onto your uphill ski early in the turn . . ." But the more he coached himself, the worse he skied. As a result, he started to get angry, and to criticize himself for his mistakes: "You're leaning too far back, you jerk. Bend your knees more." The harder he tried, the more forced and strained his skiing became. The magic was gone.

Being at the peak of one's power is an incredible feeling. When it is gone, we naturally want to get it back again, but usually our very efforts to regain it only drive it further away, leaving us frustrated. Deliberate attempts to re-create effortlessness and spontaneity only achieve the opposite, raising the question: How can one attain results without trying?

Breakthrough experiences don't occur by trying to make them happen. That's not how our first such experience happened, nor how our next will. Trying to have a breakthrough experience is like trying to grab a wisp of smoke; not only can you not do it, but you will only become frustrated if you persist in the attempt. Time and again experience shows us that the part of us that tries is the *obstacle* to our true potential. It is a truly different part of us that skis our best and makes a natural effort without straining. You can increase the frequency of your breakthrough experiences if you understand more about these two parts of yourself.

SELF 1 AND SELF 2

Listen to the thoughts that stream through your mind as you ski. Most minds are active with a flow of instructions about how to do this and how to avoid doing *that*—self-criticism, self-analysis, worries, fears, and doubts. In many cases the chatter is continuous and often less than friendly. Step back for a moment and attend to these voices. Who is instructing, criticizing, and doubting whom? A person might answer, "I'm just talking to myself." Fine, but who is the "I" and who is the "myself"? Clearly they have different identities, or else they wouldn't be conversing. There would be no need for a conversation if there was only one party, because the one speaking would already know what was going to be said and so have no need to say it. That's why when we're at one with ourselves there is no internal dialogue and we experience inner peace.

In following the Inner Game approach, recall that the voice doing all the talking, judging, worrying, and doubting is coming from Self 1, and that it is instructing Self 2, you, your body, and all its inherent potential, the one that performs all the actions. Self 1 is the ego mind that has to be in control, so it tells you how or how not to ski, that you are hopeless or great, that you are better than Joe, but not as good as Jim, and so forth. In most minds, these two selves don't get along well, a condition that makes skiing one's best impossible. In fact, if Self 1 and Self 2 were actually two separate persons, their relationship would be so clearly perceived to be based on mistrust that no one would even suggest that they try to cooperate.

Although Self 1 may sound as if it is the expert in skiing and everything else, through experience we soon discover that we perform best when we are thinking least. During breakthrough runs Self 1 is in a rare state of quiet. Control shifts to the nonverbal innate guidance system within our bodies, and our actions are directed silently. Self 1 is sometimes embarrassed and humbled by the recognition that we ski best when we are "out of our minds," but more often it resists admitting that it isn't really important to our success, and that over-conceptualizing— indeed, any conscious thought at all—interferes with the expression of our highest capabilities.

Once we understand that the voice of Self 1 is not *your* voice but comes from a collection of self-concepts, doubts, and fears accumulated over a lifetime that causes breakdowns and prevents optimal skiing, we can stop blaming our equipment, other people, snow conditions, and moguls. When Self 1 is in a quiet state, our awareness increases and we discover Self 2, that part of us that can respond to any situation instanta- neously with its fullest capabilities. Self 2, our innate potential, already exists within each of us: we catch a glimpse of it every time we experi- ence a breakthrough. Hence, the main objective of the Inner Game is to free ourselves of whatever inner obstacles prevent Self 2's fullest expres- sion and development.

WHO IS SELF 2?

Although it isn't easy to conceptualize the difference between Self 1 and Self 2, it isn't difficult to detect the difference in skiing performed under these two influences. When we asked an Inner Skiing clinic at Copper Mountain to come up with words that describe skiing under Self 1's con- trol in contrast with Self 2's the following words were used:

Self 1	Self 2
Trying	Free
Tense	Exhilarated
Mechanical	Light
Bored	Flowing
Unsure	Smooth
Scared	Relaxed
Distracted	Effortless
Struggling	Gravity
Thinking	Powerful
Expectant	Quiet
Angry	Swift
Heavy	Surprised
Hesitant	Soft
Choppy	Magical
Preconceiving	Flying
Holding Back	Rhythmic
Confused	Floating
Oh, my God!	Ecstatic

Think of all the actions that must be performed simply to turn your skis: shifting weight to the outside leg, bending the knee and ankle forward and laterally to increase edge control, moving your shoulder, arm, and hand to plant your pole, shifting your weight by stepping onto the uphill ski—and countless other movements too numerous and subtle to describe. Any movement we make in skiing—or in anything else, for that matter—requires literally hundreds of instantaneous instructions from the nervous system to different muscle groups in our bodies.

Who is doing all this? Whoever, it is certainly a lot more sophisticated and competent than a nagging Self 1 who, thinking it is in control, keeps yelling, "Bend your knees, stupid!" Just who is being stupid?

Self 2 is the name we give to the total potential that exists within each of us. In his book *On Physical Education* the Indian scholar Sri Aurobindo described what we call Self 2 as "the essential and instinctive body consciousness which can see and do what is necessary without any mental thought . . . it is equivalent in the body to swift insight in the mind and spontaneous and rapid decision in the will." But there is nothing innately spiritual or mystical about Self 2 that makes it magically appear at certain moments. It is always within us, and it expresses itself to the extent that we can ignore the interference of the mind, Self 1. Self 2 is the basic intelligence that includes the central nervous system, the brain, and other parts of our sensory apparatus we don't even know about. Whatever we do—each movement we make, each word we speak—is too complex an operation to be controlled by our conscious mind.

Self 1 could never learn the multitude of instructions necessary for even the simplest such task, much less communicate them instantaneously to our muscles. Therefore Self 2 expresses itself not just during breakthrough runs, but also in the most mundane activities: washing dishes, hammering a nail, getting dressed, eating. The complexities involved are truly amazing. Consider the act of hammering a nail. Initially you must exert pressure with the fingers of one hand to position the nail in place, then grip the hammer with the fingers of your other hand, flexing the forearm enough to keep the grip firm but not so hard as to lose flexibility. Next you must tighten the biceps to bend your elbow and rotate your shoulder to raise your arm while cocking your wrist at the top of the swing. All this and more just in order to get the hammer in position before bringing it down on the head of the nail! Then comes the amazingly complex hand-eye coordination that guides the hammer to the nailhead. Self 1 could never learn by itself to do the least complicated of these actions.

The fullest expression of Self 2 usually occurs during early childhood, before we accumulate limiting and distorted self-concepts. The child learns and performs with a minimum amount of Self 1 interference, which is why his movements look so natural, no matter what his level of proficiency. If a child started "trying too hard," criticizing himself for his lack of progress and thinking about how he moved, we would think it very unnatural. It would be—and it is just as unnatural when we do it as adults. It seems normal only because we've done it for so long that we've grown accustomed to it.

WHO IS SELF 1?

You can find the answer to this question by taking a moment to listen to the almost interminable stream of thoughts inside your head. On the mountain Self 1 may be squawking some of the following:

"Bend your knees."

"Keep your weight on your downhill ski."

"That was a lousy turn. You didn't edge enough."

"You'll never learn."

"You're too uncoordinated for this sport."

"You'll never be any good."

"This slope is too steep for you."

"Look at those moguls! You'll wipe out for sure."

"Don't be a chicken. If those turkeys can do it so can you."

"Keep your skis together and try to look good under the chair lift."

Obviously Self 1 thinks it knows all the answers because it is always telling you how to ski, evaluating and judging your progress, criticizing your mistakes, doubting your ability and comparing it with others', warning and worrying about failing and falling. In sum, Self 1 is an extremely complex character who plays a lot of different roles. Some of these are:

THE INSTRUCTOR He is constantly telling you everything you should be doing, how you should do it, and when. "Keep your weight on your downhill ski . . . No, not that much, you'll lose your balance . . . Now shift your weight to the inside edge of your outside ski and roll your ankles across the fall line . . ." Afraid that nothing will go right if he's not talking, the Instructor loves to repeat his dictum: "Bend your knees, bendyourknees, bendyurnees!" Not only is he convinced that you can't learn to ski without him, but he also assumes that you have a very short memory! If I had to pay for all the instructions my Self 1 gives me, I couldn't afford the price of a lift ticket.

HELPLESS HARRY The opposite of the Instructor, Helpless doesn't trust you to be able to do anything for yourself. He always foresees problems, and wants to ask for help, advice, or information, whether you need it or not. Instead of urging you to get up when you fall, and to put your own ski back on, he advises you to lie in the snow until somebody stops. If you follow Helpless's advice, you become overly dependent on others, and are usually the last to get your skis on and the last one down the slope.

Like Laurel and Hardy, Helpless and the Instructor make a great pair: one thinks he knows everything and is constantly giving instructions; the other thinks he knows nothing and is constantly seeking them.

FLASHY FRED is not as concerned with how well you ski as with how well you look. Continually worried about what others think of you, he cripples you through self-consciousness and urges you to impress on-lookers with your flashiest form. His ultimate high is to have you ski under the lift so that everyone can see you—provided, of course, that the trail isn't too difficult. But without spectators to applaud you, Flashy Fred has all the motivation of a leaky balloon.

THE COMPETITOR is always comparing your skiing with someone else's, urging you to try to ski faster and farther than those around you. He also wants you to know the fastest route to the mountain and how to get the best deal on equipment. Jaw tightened in determination, he feels betrayed if you ever want simply to relax and enjoy yourself.

FEARFUL is obsessed with falling and failing, and is afraid of bruising both your body and your ego. His favorite phrase is "Uh-oh, here comes. . . ." His second favorite is "I can't ski this!" His tension as he searches for signs of disaster is contagious, spreading tightness through-out your body, making you look as wooden as a statue on skis.

FEARLESS is bored skiing a slope within your competence. He loves risk and hates speeds that are under control. For him the perfect run is to flirt with disaster from the top of the mountain to the bottom. As he makes you fly down expert slopes looking as if you're going to crash and burn at any moment, his recklessness imperils not only yourself but almost everyone else.

THE KLUTZ is convinced that when God was handing out coordination, you dropped it. He knows beforehand that you will fail at anything ath-letic, and just to make sure that this occurs he constantly tells you what an awkward, slow learner you are. He also feels it important to tell every-one else how uncoordinated you are, just in case someone expects you to be able to ski. What frightens Klutz most is your having a good run when someone is looking; it destroys the self-image he has set up for you.

THE CRITIC has something negative to say about everything you do. Even if your turn is 99 percent perfect, he'll focus on the 1 percent error. His high standards aren't as annoying as his refusal to admit your current ability. He doesn't want you to become expert because it would put him out of a job.

Perhaps in the above you've recognized some of your own Self 1 roles. Here are a few others: Julius Judge, Horatio Hero, Nervous Nellie, Top Sergeant, Ego Tripper, Harriet Helper.

One word of caution. We can become so involved with the task of identifying and analyzing various Self 1 disguises that we neglect our skiing. This is simply one more of Self 1's roles—the Analyst. He gets us thinking so much about the cause of a bad turn or fall, or even how to cope with another Self 1 persona, that we lose touch with the present experience.

Self 1 would have us believe that he is indispensable to skiing and life, but in fact his constant chatter interferes with performance. This becomes apparent when we remember how quiet and thought-free the mind is when we are performing at our best. During a breakthrough run the mind is not directing, criticizing, judging, analyzing, or being fearful; instead, it is quietly focused on the present.

One Self 1 role that frequently emerges to sabotage my own skiing is Flashy Fred, who wants me to impress onlookers. Typically he takes over when I am skiing under the chair lift. At the beginning of a run I am paying attention only to my skiing; then suddenly I become aware of the people overhead riding the lift. Foolishly I imagine that they are all looking at me, and my concentration switches from my skiing to them. But when I'm on stage, with the lift riders as my audience, I usually don't ski as well, and often attract their attention only with a spectacular crash.

Self 1's demands on our attention rob us of the energy needed to see the slope clearly or to feel movement and our skis. It is because of this limited awareness that we make mistakes, lose control and fall more often. The worse we ski, the more we strain, and this in turn causes tightness and awkwardness, resulting in further loss of balance and control. "See," Self 1 then shouts triumphantly. "You're not good enough for this slope." Thus the mental stress translates directly into physical movements.

This connection between thought and action has been described well by Dr. Roberto Assagioli in *The Act of Will:* "Images, mental pictures and ideas tend to produce the physical conditions and the external acts that correspond to them."

Self 1's basic goal is to ensure its own survival and continuing influence over your skiing and your life. To this end it will even go so far as to pretend to undertake the project of getting rid of itself. After reading this chapter, for instance, you may grow impatient with your foibles and shortcomings, frustrated at not allowing Self 2 to be in charge more often, and hence chastise yourself whenever Self 1 is in control. But instead of judging your skiing, now you are judging yourself for being judgmental and for not playing the Inner Game well! Instead of straining to ski well, you now strain to be in the present moment and try hard to not try hard! Thus Self 1 is perpetuated and retains control indefinitely. We call this Self 1 persona the New Age Judge. He tells us how we should *be* rather than how we should *ski*. Sly, isn't he? He has an inexhaustible set of disguises, so dealing with him requires that first we must be able to recognize him before we can tame him.

Self 1 is stronger than we think, and not easy to silence. Its different roles are like wild horses that we let pull us in many directions all day long. Then when we decide to use them for a single goal we grow frustrated because they won't pull in unison and respond to our commands. We all would like our minds to stay quietly in the present when we ski, but can we keep from worrying about the next turn or criticizing the one we just made? Few believe that their fears and self-doubts are really helpful, but can we silence them? To what extent do we control the reins of our own thoughts?

If we try to fight Self 1 head-on, we find ourselves in a battle that we can't possibly win. We create an interminable civil war in our heads that is diametrically opposite to the state of peace we are seeking. Ultimately, the mind is controlled not by fighting with it but by taming it, by gradually regaining our rightful authority over our own thoughts, so that instead of letting them take us where they want to go, we set the direction. The entire process of the Inner Game described in these pages is directed toward the simple goal of quieting Self 1 so that Self 2 is free to express its true abilities and chosen direction.

The process of regaining your mastery over Self 1 starts with the simple recognition of its existence. Yet we must also realize that Self 1 is not who we really are. When we observe the thoughts and roles of the mind, we know that we and the thoughts are different. By observing Self 1 nonjudgmentally, we no longer identify with it; we simply watch it. As soon as I see Flashy Fred for who he is, I can separate myself from him and can choose to refocus my attention on my skiing. Separating from Self 1 is like being aware that a dream, while it is still going on, is only a dream; as a result, the illusion no longer has the same power or control over us. Similarly, the degree to which we can step back from Self 1 and no longer be subject to its doubts, fears, and desires is the measure of our success in taming it. As we approach this goal, Self 2 will become more apparent and will have an easier time expressing itself.

TAMING SELF 1

The Inner Game approach to releasing our potential involves two basic steps: quieting Self 1 and trusting Self 2. These two skills go hand in hand, and each is necessary in order to achieve success. The reason Self 1 is so active is that it doesn't trust the abilities of Self 2. Else, why all those repeated instructions? In skiing, trusting Self 2 means allowing it to control the movements of your body. This doesn't mean that if a beginning skier trusts his body he will immediately ski like an expert; what it does mean is letting the body do what it already can and trusting that it will learn how to do what it can't yet do.

Why should we trust Self 2? Simply because it is more trustworthy than Self 1 in terms of both performance and ability to learn, as all of us

TRUSTING SELF 2

have discovered on breakthrough runs. Another word for trusting Self 2 is confidence, which is nothing more than Self 1's recognition of the amazing abilities of Self 2. It is commonly recognized that confidence is essential to high-level performance, but not so commonly understood is how we come by this elusive quality. Trusting our own potential is at once an act of the will and a process. Consider the example of a father teaching his fifteen-year-old son to drive a car. Intellectually he may decide to trust his son, but *confidence* in him will develop only when, over a period of time, the son's driving skills give evidence that the trust is well placed. At first the father may trust his son to drive only in an empty parking lot, and then on a country road. Certainly he doesn't give the boy the keys and let him loose on the freeway, any more than a responsible ski instructor will lead a beginner down an advanced run. Trust is important, but it should be given to the individual skier according to his ability and the situation. If the father teaching his son to drive is constantly barking instructions to him, and even grabs the wheel himself whenever another car comes in sight, little learning will take place and there is little chance for confidence to grow. Similarly, when we don't trust ourselves to learn from experience, we seriously hamper our development.

We will never learn whether or not Self 2 is reliable unless we allow it to take control, and if we allow Self 1 to reassert itself every time we make a mistake, we will never discover Self 2's ability to correct itself. Regaining confidence in Self 2 takes time, but the process can't even begin unless we *decide* to trust it and give it a chance to show what it can do. Whenever we are doubtful of Self 2's ability to learn to ski, we can ask ourselves to remember how we instinctively corrected ourselves after our falls when we were learning to walk at about the age of a year.

The remainder of this book is about how to increase our ability to quiet the interferences of the mind and to develop a recognition of, and trust in, our innate abilities to perform and learn.

3 ✳
NATURAL
LEARNING
IS SENSE-ABLE

Dick, a close friend, recently came to visit me. He hadn't been on the slopes for a few years and had decided to take his children on a week-long skiing trip. Eager to teach his youngest son, Ben, who was six years old, he asked, "How do you go about teaching someone that age?"

"The most important thing to remember is not to try to teach him too much," I answered. "Make sure he's warm and comfortable and, above all, let him have fun. The rest will take care of itself. Don't give him too many instructions—in fact, the fewer the better." I also told him about a few games he could play with Ben as they skied together.

A few weeks later Dick dropped by again, and I asked him about the trip. "You should have seen Ben," he said. "He's a natural! He just bombed down the beginners' slope the first day as if he'd been doing it his whole life. He was even turning pretty well, without more than a hint from me. He fell once in a while but it didn't bother him at all—he'd just get up and go at it again."

"I felt pretty rusty," Dick continued, "so one morning I decided to take a lesson. My instructor was a really hot skier and seemed to be a good teacher, but I guess I wasn't that good a student. I really had a hard time. I tried to remember his instructions, and if I'd been able to get my body to do what I was telling it, I'd have been in good shape. As it was, I found it frustrating. No matter what I did, I couldn't seem to regain my old form. Later, when I saw Ben skiing so effortlessly I got a headache—I was having so much trouble doing something that supposedly I already knew how to do and there he was, skiing so easily his first time out. Though he hadn't acquired any refinements yet, there was a naturalness to his skiing that I envied—plus the fact that he was enjoying himself so much."

The main difference between Ben's and Dick's learning experience was their state of mind. Dick was continually *thinking* about how to ski, while Ben was just doing it. Dick's mind was busy trying to understand the right way to turn, consciously directing his body through it step by step, and then analyzing the results. After each "mistake" he criticized himself harshly and strained even harder. Ben, on the other hand, watched what others were doing and simply imitated them. He wasn't trying to analyze how to turn, or worrying about doing it the right way or about looking good. Since he was just out to ski and have fun, he did both without strain, whereas Dick was trying too hard to have fun and too busy talking to himself to learn much.

How often have you watched—with a mixture of wonder and resentment—"those damn kids" on their little skis shoot down the beginners' slope, weaving in and out between older beginners? The first time they strap on a pair of skis, children seem to have an innate sense about the sport. While the rest of us are still stiffly snowplowing our way across a slope, they have been up and down it five times.

Children are natural learners. Psychologists and learning theorists tell us that we learn more in our first five years than we are apt to absorb during the rest of our lives. Why? Do children know something that we don't? Have we forgotten something we once knew?

Children learn faster because they don't think they know anything to start with. Ben didn't have any preconceived ideas about the right way to ski. He simply went out on a slope, watched others, and tried to duplicate what he saw, letting his body find out what worked best. His mind was clear and open to discovery.

Dick's mind, on the other hand, was too full of the rights and wrongs, the do's and don'ts of skiing, to be open to learning. Talking his way down the mountain, he skied more with his head than with his body. All his self-instructions prevented him from experiencing his skis and his body.

I remember attending as an adolescent one of those dance classes where we learned the box step by moving our feet from one footprint to the next, chanting "Forward, across, together, back, across, together . . ." After practicing to this rigid cadence, music was finally played and we were expected to pick out a partner and start dancing. However, any similarity between what I was doing and real dancing was purely coincidental. I would step all over my partner's feet as I counted "One, two, three, forward, back, together," making sure that my feet were in the "right" place.

Most adults try to learn by memorizing a series of individual actions to create one whole movement. Hence, their approach to skiing is to follow footprints in their minds. Initially they look outside themselves—perhaps a magazine article, an instructor, or a not-so-knowledgeable friend—for a set of concepts of the "right" way to ski. They focus their attention on those concepts, doing everything they can to follow them, not realizing that by intellectualizing the process they are stifling the sense of their bodies' movements. Ben did exactly the opposite, which is why he learned so easily.

When I was a beginner, the "correct" way to ski was to keep your legs tightly pressed together with your boots touching. In all the instructional manuals the emphasis was on making parallel turns and keeping the body in this position. If you had your skis close together, you were good; if not, thumbs down. All my efforts were guided by this concept of how I *should* be skiing, and I never focused on how my body responded to it or whether it actually worked for me or not. At first, it felt uncomfortable and unnatural. But I wasn't concerned with how my body was feeling because I wanted so badly to do it *right*. After years of forcing my legs and skis into this position, the discomfort was almost unnoticeable—not because it became natural but because it became habit. I was aware not of how I felt but of how I thought I looked.

Learning by following rules, we judge our performance on the basis of how close it is to the "right" way. The conceptualized turn is good not because it feels right and works, but only because it conforms to the standard. However, if we allow a concept to guide our experience, we perform by rote, and our actions are mechanical and unnatural. Our learning is impeded because we are no longer being led by *experience* but by *ideas*. As a result, Self 2 is screened off from feeling the necessary subtleties of our actions and is therefore prevented from developing any refinements.

It is more important to feel where your skis are than to know where they should be. If you are obsessed with *shoulds* to the point of neglecting what *is*, you will soon be frustrated, angry, and discouraged—none of this will help your performance. The child, on the other hand, knows what he

CONCEP-
TUAL
LEARNING:
TRYING TO
DO IT THE
"RIGHT"
WAY

wants to do and has no preconceived notions about the right way of doing it.

"Should" is a concept of the way things aren't instead of the way they are. The player of the Inner Game often finds that the right way is the wrong way. He may use concepts to point him in a certain direction, but he relies on his experience of what feels good and at the same time works best for him. In the Inner Game the *should* emerges spontaneously as we increase our awareness of *is.*

Many people, myself included, were guided for years by the *shoulds* of parents, friends, and society: the right way of doing things, the right profession, the right lifestyle, the right relationship. Rather than letting our own intuition, awareness, and interests guide our choices, we conformed, but many of us failed to find fulfillment.

EXPERIEN-TIAL LEARNING

Billy's mother points to the fireplace and says, "See that fire? Be careful of it because it's very hot and can burn you badly. Stay away from it!" Tommy's mother leads him close to the fire, holds his hand out toward it, and says, "Now, move a little closer." Tommy does so, but stops at the point where the heat becomes too uncomfortable. "Hot," his mother says as he withdraws his hand. "Fire is hot, and if you get too close it burns you."

On being *told* about the dangers of fire, the first child tucks the idea into his mind and has to remind himself whenever he is near fire not to get close to it. By being allowed to *feel* the heat and discover the danger for himself, Tommy *knows* through experience that fire is hot and he will exercise caution. Billy learned only that his mother didn't want him near the fire, while Tommy learned that the danger of the heat depended on how close he came to the fire. Billy learned to fear fire, while Tommy learned to respect it, so that his mind will be open to discovering its uses and appreciating its beauty.

To have to *try* to remember something means that you don't really *know* it. Because his mind is so full of other thoughts and ideas, sooner or later Billy won't remember his mother's caution; eventually he will get a little too close, feel the heat, and *then* will learn about fire the hard way.

When you are aware of an experience, you learn at a level much deeper than that of the conceptual mind. Awareness is the Self 2 learning process, whereas conceptual learning starts and stops at Self 1. Moreover, almost any action is far more complex than any description of it. The art of skiing can't be described as the act of keeping knees bent and skis together, any more than fire can be described by just saying that it's hot. An action is a synthesis of many movements, all executed in harmony with one another. It would be impossible for the mind to learn by rote all the intricacies of movement involved in turning your skis, let

32

alone sending all those instructions simultaneously to the muscles of your body so that you can accomplish that turn.

Self 2 learns by discovery—by *doing* rather than *thinking about doing.* Like an explorer, Self 2 always perceives its environment as virgin territory. With a childlike curiosity, it is open and attentive to whatever it may encounter. It may have a preliminary idea of where it wants to go and what it wants to accomplish, but it is free of constricting expectations of how its goal must be achieved or what it will find on its way.

Self 2 lets experience be the guide. Remaining objective and interested, it grows by absorbing what is happening from moment to moment. In the process of discovery it senses and observes, constantly picking up information and making appropriate adjustments in its actions and direction, thus becoming increasingly able to cope with the situation at hand. The natural learning process is discovery by experience.

When exposed to an unfamiliar skill, children will watch what is going on for a few minutes with total concentration. Wide-eyed, they simply gawk, absorbing the entire image at once without breaking it down into its separate parts. It is because children don't segment experience that they are such superb mimics.

The adult, on the other hand, tends to see movement in terms of a series of stop-action poses which he then translates into a list of instructions to himself. "Oh, I see—he edges his downhill ski, plants his pole, stops onto the uphill ski, and rides it through the turn." Even if he were to succeed in forcing his body to comply with these instructions, he would miss much of what a skiing turn is. A turn is more than just the sum of its parts; it includes rhythm, grace, balance, and coordination—none of which is on Self 1's list. Skiing by the numbers usually results in moving like a robot through the turn.

A child doesn't learn linearly; he learns holistically. With a quiet and open mind, he takes in whole images: not just visual images, but "feelages" as well. With his concentration focused, he acquires a *feel* for what he is *seeing.* Self 2 then creates corresponding kinesthetic sensations in his body, so that he is almost duplicating the movement as he watches it. Free of self-judgments, when he begins to move he imitates what he saw. Totally involved in his actions, his senses continually feed back detailed information from the experience.

A baby may fall when first attempting to walk, but when he does, his body absorbs all the details of the fall. Without concepts of any kind, his Self 2 automatically adjusts the next step he takes, making it longer or shorter, straightening the position of the head to correct for imbalance. As his body continues to receive more detailed information with each

33

succeeding step, it is able to refine the new movement. Only because his mind is quiet enough to feel the subtle sensations that tell him when he is on or off balance does any learning take place.

This demonstrates a basic principle of the Inner Game, and the essence of the natural learning process: *the quality of learning is directly proportionate to the quality of feedback one receives from experience.* A mind that is busy worrying, criticizing, and comparing will block feedback, just as a clogged filter will prevent air from flowing through it. The more active the mind, the less feedback the body will receive, and the slower it will learn. The key to natural learning is to quiet the Self 1 mental activity so that awareness is increased.

BODY AWARE- NESS

While skiing, we get visual feedback from the terrain and aural feedback from the sounds our skis make on the snow. However, we learn most from our awareness of the movements of the body. Learning increases in direct proportion to our ability to focus on this.

What does body awareness mean? Try this simple exercise and experience it for yourself. Raise your right hand over your head. Then lower it. Raise it a second time, but this time notice how it feels as you are lifting it. Experience your hand lowering again. What was the difference between the two sets of movement? Lift your arm a third time with your eyes shut so you can more easily focus on the feeling. How can you tell that your arm is actually moving? What sensations indicate the location of your arm at each moment? Can you distinguish between the sensations of upward and downward movements? If you pay close attention, you will feel some muscles tighten while others relax at the moment the arm changes directions. See if you can locate those muscles that contract in order to raise the arm. Can you feel them let go as the arm lowers?

The more attentive and relaxed the mind, the more able it is to pick up increasingly minute muscle and energy sensations in the body. Continue the exercise with other parts of the body. You will find that the more attentive the mind grows, the more subtle sensations it will pick up.

Frequently, after a skier makes a few turns and I ask him what he experienced, the answer comes back in terms of what *wasn't* experienced. For example: "I didn't plant my pole right."

"How do you know you didn't plant your pole right?"

"Because it didn't feel right."

"What did you actually feel that told you it wasn't right?"

"My arm felt rigid and my shoulder was tight."

"Aha! Then *that's* the experience. You felt the rigidity in your arm and the tightness in your shoulder. Everything else you reported was only thinking."

Awareness is experiencing something directly; *thinking* is conceptualizing about what we are experiencing. They are two critically different processes. The more we think about an experience, the less aware we become of the experience itself. Once again: *as thinking increases, awareness decreases.*

If, while listening to a person who is talking to me, I look at him directly and attend to his words, I will be aware of the essential communication between us. But if I am wondering how he feels about me, or if I am busily preparing my reply to what he is saying, I am obviously not going to be aware of what is being communicated by him.

One day Tim Gallwey was asked to demonstrate to a group of ski instructors how Inner Game principles might be applied to the teaching of novice skiers. First he observed a beginners' class as it was being taught, and then he was given a class of twelve students who had never been on skis before. It would be his first group of students off the tennis courts, and he was obviously looking forward to the experiment.

The first step with beginners at this particular school was to teach them how to side-step up a hill. Tim followed this procedure, but gave no instructions about how each step should be done. Once the class had their skis on, he simply asked the students to get used to the extensions on their feet while standing still. He suggested that they shift their weight from one foot to the other, move them up and down and sideways, bend and straighten their knees, and edge and flatten their skis. Each pupil explored in his own way what it was like to wear skis. There were no rights or wrongs, simply the exploration of something new. After a few minutes Tim said, "Follow me," and started side-stepping up the gentle slope. Before the novices could start worrying about whether they were following him "correctly," Tim started talking. "The first thing I want you to become aware of is your skis. As you move up the hill, are they flat or edged into the snow? Don't look at mine and don't look at your own. I simply want you to feel them."

The students immediately stopped *trying* to side-step and began to become aware of their skis. As they progressed up the hill, each of them could tell that his skis were edged into the snow. Then, partway up the slope, Tim stopped them and asked them to play with their edges some more. "Without looking at them, see what happens when you flatten your skis." As the students did so, they all began to slide a little downhill, then automatically edged to stop themselves. "That's why you were all edging as you side-stepped," he said. "Who told you how to do that? I didn't; yet everyone did it. In a traditional class, you might have been told to remember to edge your skis, and you probably would have tried hard

Two Examples

to do it 'right.' But now you are doing it automatically without thinking about it. Something in you is pretty smart, and as you learn to ski you will grow to trust it more and more.

"Next, I want you to edge your skis as much as you possibly can..... We'll call that amount of edging a five. Now a little less—that's four—still less—that's three—and perfectly flat will be zero. Now as we continue to side-step up the hill, I want each of you to call out the number that corresponds to the degree that you feel your skis are edged into the snow. There's no correct number; just feel how much they are edged, step by step, and call out the number. Remember, no fair looking—just do it by feel." As the students started up the slope, calling out numbers, it was easy to see that their concentration had increased. There was no anxiety in their voices, simply absorption in what they were feeling. At first the numbers varied from about one to four, but after a while each student seemed to have found his particular number. At the top of the rise Tim stopped the class and asked each member to report the amount of edging he was using most. Most had settled on a two or three, and one girl asked if three was "best." "I don't know which number is best," said Tim. "How did you find that three worked?" "Oh, it worked fine," said the girl. "I just didn't know if it was right." Tim's comment was, "It's obviously right for you at this moment."

Everyone looked relieved that this hadn't been a test. They seemed to be getting the idea that this teacher trusted them to discover what worked best for each of them. Without really trying they had already learned side-stepping, simple control of skis, and a basic awareness of edging that would form a foundation for their skiing.

I saw how simple yet universally applicable this principle of body awareness was the next day, when Tim was working with a group of advanced skiers. Among these was Peter Kronig, an instructor from Zermatt, who had been teaching skiing for twenty years. Four of us took a run down an intermediate slope with no instruction other than to be aware of our bodies and to notice which part held our attention the most. After skiing half the run, each of us reported what we had focused on. My attention had centered on my knees as I had become interested in the extent they were bending on each turn. Tim had been most aware of the rotation of his shoulders. When it was Peter's turn to report, he seemed slightly bored. "Vell, I am alvays avare ov my edges ven I ski," he said. He seemed so competent and self-assured that I began to wonder if Inner Skiing could possibly offer him anything.

Then Tim said that he wanted to pay even closer attention to his shoulders, and suggested that each of us simply increase our awareness of the part of our bodies that had come to our attention. I was amused when he suggested to Peter exactly what he had told the class of beginners the day before. "Peter, you seem to focus on your edges, but why don't you see if you can increase your awareness. Call the maximum amount of edging ten and zero for flat. As you take each turn call out to yourself the number that seems right to you."

When we collected at the bottom of the slope, Peter was so excited that I could hardly understand all that he said. "It vas vonderful! I never felt quite like that. I could tell such little differences. Ven I vas at seven it was like pure light, and then ven I unedged at zero, the darkness was there. It vas beautiful."

The reference to light and darkness puzzled us, but we could all tell that Peter, who had skied all his life and seemed beyond any surprise, was now like a kid with a new toy. He was discovering the secret of awareness, and how it makes all experience fresh. What we all found out was that simple body awareness is the same for everyone. We never outgrow it. Only the degree of subtlety increases.

FEEDBACK FROM RESULTS

Natural learning depends on more than feedback from the body; it also depends on what *works*. Not all the moves in skiing will feel natural at first because our bodies were designed for walking and running, not for sliding across snow at high speeds. When working with the beginners, Tim emphasized focusing not only on the subtle sensations of the body but also on results. He encouraged them to be able to feel the difference between a three and a zero edge, and also to observe the different *effects* of each amount of edging.

Only by getting accurate feedback from both the feel of muscle movements and the results of these movements can Self 2 make the appropriate corrections. If the skier is trying too hard to attain certain results, it will be far more difficult for him to feel those that he is achieving, which in turn will interfere with the correction process. If he makes a certain movement that causes him to fall, he needn't try to make a conscious correction. If he felt both the movement causing the imbalance and the resulting fall, the automatic learning process of Self 2 will make the correction. Although this may be hard to believe for those who have become used to trusting only their conscious Self 1, a little experimenting will prove that the body really does know how to correct itself if it is given the necessary feedback.

When Tim is teaching tennis students to hit targets with their serve, he always says that it's not necessary to *try* to hit the target; rather, what is important is to see exactly where each serve lands in relation to the target. If the student misses the target by five feet to the right, he isn't asked to aim farther to the left, but he is simply told to serve again without consciously trying to make any correction. His Self 2 is trusted to do the correcting. Self 1 is always surprised when it sees how soon the body learns to hit the target without its help.

The same principle is applicable to skiing. I need to feel what happens when my skis flatten coming out of a turn, when they are slightly edged, and when they are more edged. By increasing awareness of both my edging and its effects on the quality of the turn, Self 2 soon discovers the optimum relationship between the two. Since there is such a wide range in terrain and speed, this optimum relationship will vary greatly.

One might well ask, "But what is the *target* in skiing?" Although the desirable goal in skiing may not be as clear-cut as in sports like tennis and golf where you keep score, it can still be recognized. To maintain *balance* while skiing—on any terrain and at any speed—is one of many ways to describe the target. Balance is necessary in all movement and the body has a particularly strong desire to achieve it when skiing. It knows much better than the conceptual mind, Self 1, how to achieve this goal.

AWARE-NESS INCREASES CONTROL

Many skiers assume that if they neglect technical information in favor of increasing body awareness, they will sacrifice proficiency. But the reverse is true. The complex feedback we get from awareness of our bodies is much more subtle and refined than the most carefully worded verbal instructions. Who can describe in words the exact amount of edging that produces the most effective turn in a given situation? The language of the body is simply too specific and sophisticated to be put into words. But we can learn that language, if we listen to our bodies, and attend to the subtleties of our kinesthetic sensations.

Increasing our ability to focus on our body sensations while skiing takes some practice. The primary purpose of the exercise is to quiet Self 1, to limit conscious thought, and to feel what is happening to our bodies. There are many ways to facilitate this process. Below are two that I have found beneficial.

A few years ago, while I was skiing at Lake Eldora, Tom Walker, the ski school director, asked me to try taking a few turns with my eyes closed. I looked around. The area was relatively flat and nobody was in sight, so I nervously agreed. But when I tried it I was so tense and afraid that all I was aware of was my mind racing in panic. Self 1 kept saying, "Watch out! You're heading for trouble!" As a result, I took only two cautious turns before opening my eyes and smiling sheepishly.

"Want to try again?" Tom asked. "It usually takes a few times to get accustomed to it."

This time I was more able to relax, and soon I became acutely aware of my feet. They seemed at one with my skis, and I could actually feel each minute change in the terrain beneath them. Even after I opened my eyes, this increased sense of awareness stayed with me, and it led to a degree of control I had never before achieved. I became aware of the slightest change in angle my edges made, my body seemed to know just how much to edge, and I was carving turns with greater precision and less effort than I had ever imagined possible.

Later Tom suggested that I take a run with my boots unbuckled. I was surprised because I had always thought that one's boots needed to be tight in order to gain maximum control. Somewhat skeptical, I started out tentatively, but it turned out to be a valuable experience. I was prevented from making any sudden movements to execute a turn because my feet would have come out of my boots; it became necessary to focus more on the soles of my feet and allow them to control my skis. I noticed how much more aware I was of the slightest change in pressure, and noticed how much control I achieved by attending to these subtle differences. Barely moving my body, simply by pressuring my feet, I could make the skis do almost anything I wanted.

In some segments of Japanese and Chinese society, small children are introduced to one or another of the martial arts, which emphasize alertness to subtle body sensations. In t'ai chi ch'uan, for instance, every movement is made carefully and slowly in order to increase one's awareness of actions and of the delicate flow of energy throughout the body. A t'ai chi master attains an amazing level of agility and control, the inevitable and natural by-products of awareness.

In our own culture, achievement is valued over awareness, as though they were independent of each other, when in point of fact body awareness is directly related to body achievement. In any sport the athletes who possess an acute ability to focus on the discrete signals of their bodies—for example, the fine line between balance and imbalance, timing and mistiming, being too tight and too loose—are those who achieve excellence.

The will to strive for higher levels of achievement is valuable, and has been the greatest spur to the development of sports in the Western world, but I feel that we have so overstressed our emphasis on this goal that a reassessment in favor of awareness is needed. Pure awareness without the will to achieve lacks direction, but the will to achieve without awareness is strained and lacks the requisite refinement to attain the highest levels of excellence. The human body is a magnificent instrument that constantly sends us subtle messages; if heeded, these would keep us healthy and allow us to perform at our highest level. But when we become too goal-oriented and anxious about the results of our actions, we begin to lose touch with our bodies. When we lack awareness of its messages, immediately our performance suffers.

To increase control over one's body, we must resist any tendency to force change. In the Inner Game approach to learning, growth begins by increasing our awareness of that which we wish to change.

Through heightened awareness, people have learned to achieve surprising degrees of control over their bodies—to slow down their heartbeat, decrease their blood pressure, and hasten their digestion. I once participated in an experiment whose goal was to raise the temperature of one's fingertips. My fingers were hooked up to a galvanic skin-response meter. Attempting to increase their temperature, I concentrated on thinking about the sun shining on my fingers, and then of putting my hands in a furnace. The result was a *decrease* of five points. Next I imagined putting my fingers in hot water, and then I tried to send heat to them through my bloodstream. Nothing worked.

The experimenter came over to me and asked, "Can you feel the temperature your hands are at now?"

"No."

"Start with that and see what happens."

Closing my eyes, I shifted my attention to the tips of my fingers, focusing on feeling what their temperature was, rather than on trying to force it up. Soon I could feel subtle changes occurring. Although I wasn't consciously trying to reach my goal, I became aware that my fingers were starting to heat up. When I opened my eyes, the temperature had increased five points! Within a short time, I was able to increase or decrease their temperature at will.

Heightened awareness leads to increased control at all levels of skiing. The more advanced one is, the greater the need for increasingly refined awareness in order to make the fine adjustments necessary to achieve balance and control at higher speeds. Nowhere is this more evident than with racers shooting through slalom courses. Since the first five places are often separated only by tenths of a second, the competitors must ski with the highest degree of precision. Even the most minute degree of over or under edging can alter the racer's line through a gate and not only cost him the race but send him shooting off the course.

Richard Bach describes how Jonathan Livingston Seagull, having learned to dive at 214 miles an hour, realizes the importance of subtle body awareness as he tries to discover how to turn at high speed:

A single wingtip feather, he found, moved a fraction of an inch, gives a smooth sweeping curve at tremendous speed. Before he learned this, however, he found that moving more than one feather at that speed will spin you like a rifle ball. . . .

Perhaps the most important step a person can take to increase awareness of his experience, on the mountain or off, is to let go of the habit of judging himself or his skiing in terms of good and bad.

In assessing the turn you have just made, you are paying too much attention to past history, and this numbs you to what is happening in the present. In brooding over that turn, you are not feeling your body or your skis right now, and you don't see clearly the terrain in front of you. Consequently you fall a little behind, and don't react quickly enough to the feedback from the turn being made because you are not "there." When the turn is labeled "good," Self 1 congratulates you and tries to remember exactly what you did so that you can repeat it. But, of course, that is not how you made the "good" turn in the first place, nor how you will make the next. After pronouncing a turn "bad," Self 1 bawls you out, starts to analyze what went wrong, and tries to force a correction. Hence "good" is no more effective than "bad," since both judgments cause you to strain either to repeat or to remedy. Self 2 needs detailed feedback from the last turn to make its corrections—not a judgment.

If you've ever bowled, you've probably seen someone turn away disgustedly as soon as he sees that his shot is not going to hit all ten pins. He doesn't want to see how bad his ball actually was, so he learns little. Can you imagine a skier who never fell? The experiences that we call mistakes are actually valuable feedback that our bodies need in order to discriminate between what works for us and what doesn't and to make the appropriate corrections.

Errors are an integral part of the learning process, even for experts. Regardless of the level at which you ski, you will make mistakes, but you can benefit from them. What we need to eliminate is not the mistakes themselves, but our fear of making them and the consequent judgments, criticisms, and anger. By accepting errors we usually make fewer of them. Further, though we may begin by only judging our performance, we generally end up judging ourselves. Accusations have a momentum of their own. Not shifting our weight quickly enough causes a "bad" turn, which creates negative feelings and often results in a "bad" run, and this, in turn, causes more negative feelings. This can easily lead to a "bad" day, and after a few such "bad" days we conclude that we are "bad" skiers. This discouragement and frustration often lingers on long after we have left the mountain, turning us into "bad" people.

Such self-judgment distorts perception, interferes with performance, and retards our abilities to learn and perform. The skier who decides that he is having a bad day inevitably will have one. The person who decides that he has reached a plateau will stay there until he decides that he is off it.

There are no bad skiers—only skiers at different levels of physical and mental development. A flower is not "better" when it blooms than when it was a bud, it is simply at a different level of development. When we stop judging ourselves and others, we become more willing to trust ourselves and we begin to ski more freely and naturally.

As Hamlet said to Rosencrantz and Guildenstern, "There is nothing either good or bad but thinking makes it so."

MISTRUST

Another obstacle to awareness and natural learning is mistrust of one's Self 2. The more a skier doubts his natural ability, the more he will instruct himself and try hard. Also, it is difficult to be aware of feedback when Self 1 is trying to force your body to do what you doubt that it can do on its own.

Since keeping balance is essential to skiing well at all levels, it is pertinent to ask whether Self 1 or Self 2 should be entrusted with this task. We've all had the experience of catching an edge or hitting a bump and being thrown off balance. We teeter in the air, suspended in space as we ride on one ski, but then an arm or leg flies out in the opposite direction and we manage to regain our upright position. It happens so fast that we react without thinking—without even realizing what we've done. In the instant we lose our balance Self 2 automatically makes five, ten, twenty-five, or more adjustments to keep us upright. Can Self 1 direct you with that much sophistication?

ROCK DANCING

As we learn to trust the body and stop trying to control and direct it, we begin to experience amazing results.

At the last meeting of a one-year teacher-training project I was directing, our group decided to take a weeklong backpacking and climbing trip in the Sierras. We planned to climb one of the higher peaks as part of the trip. Starting out early one morning, we made it to the top by noon. It was an exhausting climb. After a picnic of wine and cheese and much elation, we started down.

At one point we hit a stretch of huge boulders and began jumping from one to the next. Gradually we picked up speed, and soon we were going so fast that there was no time to think about which rock to jump to next or how to land. We had to abandon our desire for conscious control and simply trust our bodies as we flew down the mountain. My attention was so riveted on what I was doing that there was no thought between awareness and action, between the feeling and doing. At first it was a little frightening, but when I saw that my body knew what it was doing, I began to trust it even more, and my fear gave way to exhilaration.

It was as if I was just along for the ride on a roller coaster, unable to control its momentum even if I had wanted to. I was out of my mind.

It seems a paradox that in order to gain real control we have to let go of trying to achieve control. But it simply means abandoning Self 1's control and letting Self 2 take over. As the Zen archer says, "We don't shoot the arrow; it shoots itself."

Before a skier can hope to achieve control, he must confront and overcome what is for most the greatest single mental obstacle to progress in skiing: fear.

4 ❄
FEAR OF
FALLING,
FAILING,
AND
FLYING

At an Inner Skiing workshop Tim and I were conducting we asked the three hundred participants to name the inner obstacles that most interfered with their proficiency and enjoyment of skiing, and then to rate these barriers by applauding to the degree that they shared them. Listening to the length and volume of the applause, we rated the obstacles on a scale from one to ten—ten being the most common and difficult, and one being those that presented a relatively low degree of difficulty.

Among other difficulties mentioned were negative self-image, poor concentration, trying too hard, and too many self-instructions. Most of these rated from three to seven on the applause meter. But fear got a thirteen; it went off the scale! There were very few participants who didn't feel that this emotion was at least detrimental to their skiing, and most saw it as a major problem. Some people in the audience even said that because of fear they had never before wanted to learn how to ski.

Tim's next announcement that the second part of the program would deal with this mental obstacle was met with cheers. It seemed to both of us that most of the participants were hoping for a magical cure—something that would immediately end their fear and create instant courage.

However, Tim took a more comprehensive approach. He asked, "Is all fear bad? Isn't there a kind of fear that isn't harmful, but in fact helpful? Haven't most of you been in a real emergency when, instead of panicking, you felt a rush of adrenaline, knew exactly what to do, and did it? This reaction is also called fear, but rather than hindering us, it helps us do things which in normal circumstances we think are well beyond our capabilities.

"Chased by a bull in a field, a lady who had never done anything athletic might run a hundred yards in twelve seconds and leap a four-foot fence without ever pausing to doubt that she could do it. Not until she was safe would she remember that she was a slow runner and couldn't jump fences.

"Although we call this kind of response 'fear,' it is markedly different from what happens to most of us as we stand atop a mountain, shaking in our boots as we look down at a mogul field, imagining all the different ways that we might fall. It's strange that we call these two responses by the same name. One heightens our perceptions and gives us added energy to perform beyond our normal capacities, whereas the other distorts our perceptions, tending to paralyze us and decrease our competence. We need only work at decreasing this second fear; the first is welcome."

When I was eighteen years old, I experienced vividly the contrasting effects of these two fears one summer while I was a lifeguard at Rockaway Beach on Long Island. It was the day after a hurricane and the waves were mountainous. Judging that the ocean was too dangerous for the average swimmer, the other lifeguards and I closed the beach to public swimming. Being strong swimmers ourselves, however, we decided to challenge the waves. It was a memorable experience for all of us, but especially for me. Catching one of those waves was like riding down a fifteen-foot slide with power behind it. When we were wiped out and thrown to the ocean floor, we would wait for a second while the wave passed over us and then push up toward the surface. The worst that could happen, we thought, would be a mouthful of salt water or a scraped nose.

Once, however, as I started toward the surface after a wipe-out, my legs became entangled in a safety rope that had come loose from its mooring. I struggled to free myself from it, but the rope only got tighter, making it impossible for me to work my way to the surface. I tried to use the rope to pull myself up, but just as I got my head above the surface for a gulp of air a huge wave crashed down on me, filling my mouth with water and pushing me to the bottom again.

I started to panic. I couldn't see, my lungs were bursting, and I felt my strength ebbing. I began to think I was going to drown. No matter how hard I tried, I couldn't get free of the rope. In one more desperate attempt, I yanked on it as hard as I could, but it only tightened more.

Luckily, something else suddenly took over. I felt an onrush of energy, my panic subsided, and I grew very calm. I knew I was in serious danger, but I stopped struggling blindly. Time seemed to slow and everything became clear. Without thinking, I knew intuitively what to do. Exhaling the remaining air in my lungs, I relaxed my muscles and let myself drop toward the ocean floor. As I descended I felt the rope loosen slightly around my legs, so that when I hit the bottom I was able to disentangle myself, push off strongly, and shoot to the top.

Caught in the initial fear, all my thrashing had only gotten me deeper into trouble, almost costing me my life. Even though I was in greater danger by the time the second fear took over, my mind was calmer and my efforts more appropriate to the situation. I actually had more air and more strength left than my fear had led me to believe. Once free of panic, I found it easy to free myself.

Since these two kinds of fear have such distinct effects on perception and performance, it makes sense to call them by different names and to learn to distinguish between them. Fear 2 will be examined first because it emerges only in rare or abnormal situations; also, it serves as a useful contrast to Fear 1, the primary obstacle for most skiers.

FEAR 2

When confronted with an emergency situation, the human body undergoes a series of physiological adjustments that prepare it for heightened action. Adrenaline is secreted into the bloodstream and breathing is stimulated. The chest expands and the throat relaxes to handle the increase of air intake. Pulse and blood pressure increase, as does the volume of blood sent to the muscles of the arms and legs. The liver manufactures glucose, adding fuel to the tissues, and the pupils of the eyes dilate, sharpening visual perception. In these amazing ways the body prepares itself for peak performance. This is the helpful kind of fear, and since it is wholly a function of Self 2 it will be referred to hereafter as Fear 2.

Fear 2 is the body's natural response to challenge. It can exist simultaneously with courage, and often precedes the performances of athletes, actors, race car drivers, soldiers, or anyone in a high-risk situation. I know a man of ordinary size who, responding to a cry of alarm, found his son with his leg caught under the wheel of a car. Without hesitation and with a powerful surge of energy, he lifted the front end of the car, freeing his son's leg.

Fear 2 focuses our attention in the present and lends us capabilities beyond our normal levels. Since this kind of fear is helpful to us, we need to learn not to resist it, nor to waste the energy it produces. In contrast with Self 1 stress and anxiety, which hang on and accumulate over time, Self 2 fear rises to the occasion and then disappears after the danger has passed.

Before looking at how to diminish the disenabling aspects of Fear 1, it is important to acknowledge the validity of Fear 2—especially in sports such as skiing where there is real danger. To feel some fear at the top of a ski slope is natural and useful and is not something that should be dismissed or even minimized without due consideration. If this fear deters you from taking a needless risk to life and limb, it is doing you a big favor and should be duly acknowledged. It is not the act of a coward to heed such fear, but the practice of the wise. It is only the Self 1 fears that are based in illusion that need to be seen through and thus dissipated.

FEAR 1

The fear that *is* harmful because it interferes with our ability to perform at our best originates in the imagination of Self 1, the ego mind, and so will be called Fear 1.

Fear 1 has a magnifying effect on our perceptions. When looking at danger, it greatly enlarges what it sees. Medium-sized bumps become *giant moguls*, intermediate slopes become *sheer precipices*, the possibility of falling becomes a *broken leg*.

While our perception of danger is exaggerated by seeing it through the small end of the telescope, our abilities to cope with this danger seem to shrink, as if we were looking through the opposite end. Our sense of competence is so depleted that we feel powerless to handle the situation confronting us.

The combined effects of these distortions make an intermediate skier at the top of an intermediate slope perceive it as advanced and himself as a beginner. Confused by these illusions, the skier, instead of reacting with heightened capabilities as he might under the influence of Fear 2, responds with hesitancy and overcautiousness, which can ultimately induce paralysis.

Standing at the head of a trail, the skier in the grip of Fear 1 looks down and begins to think how steep it looks. Feeling the anxiety churning in his stomach, he thinks of the times he has fallen on similar slopes or in similar conditions. He may remember a time when he was hurt and see it happening again. Instead of flexing slightly in readiness for action, his muscles react to his fear by becoming rigid and immobile. His courage ebbs, he feels weaker, and his vision blurs.

The more the skier's anxiety mounts, the more Self 1 inflates the danger and deflates his ability. If eventually he does attempt the slope, he does so with overtight muscles and in a distracted state. He is so sure that he is going to fall that indeed he does, even before moving very fast. He picks himself up embarrassed, knowing at this point that the slope wasn't difficult and that there was no need to fall. By exaggerating the danger and minimizing his own capabilities, Fear 1 caused his negative expectations to materialize.

This tendency of Fear 1 to magnify perceptions, to make things seem worse than they are, occurs in many areas of life. Many years ago I applied for a job with a New York advertising agency, and was told to wait in the reception room until I was called. Joining the other applicants and feeling very nervous, I peeked over my magazine to look at the competition. They all looked like Tom Cruise, self-assured and calm. I began to think how much better dressed and how much more professional they looked. Soon I was a nervous wreck—my hands sweating, stomach queasy—and became so caught up in the fear I had created for myself that it was difficult to be at my best when my interview took place.

The mind and the body are not separate units working independently; each affects the other. Originating in the mind, Fear 1 is immediately transmitted to the body and governs its actions.

THE EFFECT OF FEAR 1 ON OUR SKIING

Probably the most vivid examples of its results in skiing can be seen with beginners. Their most common characteristic is stiffness of movement. Their legs tend to be tight and inflexible, their knees locked, their shoulders hunched, their fists clenched tight as they hold their poles and their faces scrunched grimly. Fear 1 can transform a class of novices into petrified statues being pushed across a slope.

When muscles are overly tense, they lose flexibility and can't react smoothly to changes in the terrain. While skiing, our knees and hips are meant to act as shock absorbers, compressing to cushion the jarring effect of bumps and then returning to normal. If these shock absorbers are already compressed, they will have no flexibility with which to react to differences in the terrain. Skiing would then be like riding over a rough road in an old Jeep: every small bump reverberates through our bodies, and the larger ones bounce us off the seat, throwing us off balance.

Besides inhibiting our flexibility, the tension resulting from Fear 1 also reduces our stamina. When our bodies are tight we have to work harder: every muscle we tense or flex requires extra effort. As our energy reserves are depleted, we tire more quickly. Our reactions slow down, our sense of timing is thrown off, our muscles become exhausted, and we lose control. As a result, our self-doubts and fears build, and the cycle perpetuates itself.

On the other hand, when we are relaxed and are skiing with Self 2 effort, we employ only the necessary muscles, and no energy is wasted in the overtightness that comes from fear and forcing. The upper body—stomach, arms, shoulders, neck and face muscles—is relatively loose, and the leg muscles do most of the skiing.

Another effect of Fear 1 is that it literally takes our breath away: we tend to stop breathing. To demonstrate the effects of this, I often ask members of my classes to hold their breath while running in place as fast as they can for one minute, paying attention to how their bodies feel while doing so. Then I ask them to run in place again, at the same speed and for the same period of time, breathing normally. Holding their breaths, they tire much more quickly—literally running out of steam. Holding one's breath not only results in unnecessary tightness of the torso and face but causes loss of oxygen. In contrast, Fear 2 induces the opposite effect, increasing the oxygen intake of the body.

THE "UH-OH" EXPERI- ENCE

In *Inner Tennis*, Tim describes a common cause of error on the courts as the "uh-oh" experience. A player with a strong forehand will return with confidence a ball coming toward his right, but when he has to use his weak backhand, he says to himself, "Uh-oh." In response to this warning, his arm tightens, his racket is jerked out of its natural path, the ball is hit off center and an error results.

This self-induced failure applies to other sports as well. Take the example of someone who has skied for a year but who still thinks of himself as a beginner. The instant he pushes off downhill he feels unsure of himself and moves overcautiously. Afraid of losing the slightest degree of control, as he starts to pick up any speed he thinks, Uh-oh, I'm going too fast. To resist forward momentum he sits backward, thereby weighting the tails of his skis, which causes him to go even faster and to lose still more control. Uh-oh, here comes a fall, he thinks, sitting still further back, thus accelerating more and tightening his body in anticipation of the fall.

I knew that was going to happen! I'm a lousy skier, he says to himself, further reinforcing his negative self-image. I'm still falling all over the beginners' slope. Now he has one more memory with which to further distort his true competence and feed Fear 1. The next time he picks up speed, his fear again will cause him to tighten and lean back again for a repeat performance.

❋

Illusion-based fear operates in a simple, self-destructive cycle. We look at a mogul field and think, I'm not good enough to handle that. The moguls begin to grow in size and degree of difficulty, and this distorted perception affects the body, which tenses in anticipation of being hurt. With muscles tight, our movements are stiff, and indeed a mogul does throw us up just as we imagined it would. This distortion in performance reinforces our already distorted self-image, and the next mogul will look even larger and more difficult.

Fear 1 distorts each component of our skiing: our perception, our performance, and our self-image. Each distortion reflects its own illusions, further skewing each of the other components. This fear cycle will inevitably continue until the distortions on which it is based are broken.

Awareness Dispels Illusion

The essential difference between Fear 2 and Fear 1 is that Fear 2 is based on reality, whereas Fear 1 is based on illusion. There is only one way to dispel illusion: to increase one's awareness of reality—of what really *is.* Though there are many ways to change the *shape* of an illusion, only awareness can *eliminate* it.

Awareness is light; illusion is darkness. Nothing except light can take away darkness. Illusion means seeing things that aren't there, or not seeing things that are there. Awareness is the energy of consciousness that, when focused on reality, allows us to see only what *is.*

A young boy going to sleep is sure he sees a boogeyman in the darkened bedroom and is paralyzed with terror. This illusion has a very real power until his father, answering the boy's frightened cries, comes in and turns on the light. The boy peeks out from under his covers, looks in the direction of the boogeyman, and sees only his own clothes draped over a chair.

"I thought I saw a boogeyman," he says sheepishly.

"Well, now you can see that there's no one here," the father says as he leaves.

But the father is wrong. There *was* a boogeyman in the room: the Fear 1 in the child's imagination—which more than likely is also still alive and well in the father's. Until the inner boogeyman is confronted, the one that projects its fears onto our external reality, we all live in the dark.

How to turn on the lights? How does one go about increasing awareness of what *is* in order to decrease Fear 1?

The Three Components of Fear 1

There are three essential components in every fear situation, and Self 1 projects its illusions on any or all of them to produce Fear 1. First, there is the sense of *danger*—that is, something capable of doing harm. Second, there is the sense of *vulnerability*—that is, there is someone capable of being harmed by this danger. Third, there is a sense of *inability* on the part of the vulnerable person to overcome the danger. If any one of these three ingredients is missing, there is no fear.

In skiing, it is usually the slope that is perceived as the danger, while that which is vulnerable is the skier's body. However, if the skier knows that he is competent enough to ski the trail, there will be no fear. If the skier is incompetent but the hill is too flat to be seen as a danger, there will also be no fear. The third possibility, the skier who does not feel vulnerable to being hurt, is hard to imagine, but theoretically such an individual would also experience no fear.

Fear 1 occurs when illusion governs one or more of these basic components. It increases in proportion to the degree that it exaggerates the danger and vulnerability, or minimizes one's ability to deal with danger. The solution to Fear 1 boils down to simply increasing awareness of the realities in a given situation—that is, increasing awareness of the real danger, of one's true competence, and of one's actual vulnerability.

DISPELLING ILLUSIONARY DANGER

To dispel an illusion that either amplifies or minimizes danger, we have to learn to look the threat in the face. In tennis, Tim suggests overcoming the "uh-oh" experience by focusing on the ball's seams. When concentrating on them, the mind sees the ball, not an "uh-oh." As a result, the body doesn't overtighten, sees the ball more as it really is, simply hits it, and avoids the error.

Similarly, our greatest obstacle to increasing our awareness of danger in skiing is that we usually resist looking closely at what frightens us. The boy afraid of the boogeyman pulled his covers over his head, making it impossible for him to reject his illusion and easier for his imagination to run wild. Because we don't like to examine danger, it remains an unknown, and the unknown is always more scary. If we hope to overcome the illusions Self 1 projects, we must be willing to look openly at danger and assess its characteristics without resistance.

A good example of using awareness to decrease fear occurred in a lesson I gave to a strong intermediate skier named John, who felt that moguls were his nemesis. He wanted to overcome this fear—especially of the moguls on a run called Big Bumps. However, when we reached the top of the run, John took one look down the slope and panicked.

"I should know better than to try this," he exclaimed. "I'm scared to death just looking down there, much less trying to ski it." His voice had a finality that seemed to say, "Forget it! Let's try another slope."

"I don't care whether we take this run or not," I said, "but as long as we're here, let's try an experiment. It involves simply looking at the slope; I promise I won't ask you to ski it."

"Okay," John agreed reluctantly. "What do you want me to do?"

"Look at the slope as if you didn't hate it and tell me what you see."

"It's damned steep!" John said immediately. "And I hate moguls. I can't help it! Too many of them have tripped me up."

"Which ones do you hate the most?" I asked.

"Those right there where it's almost straight down," he answered, pointing to the steepest part of the slope.

"Take your ski pole," I suggested, "and use it as a plumb line to estimate the angle of that part of the trail. Be as accurate as you can. How many degrees off the horizontal is it?"

After a pause, John looked up surprised, his pole still dangling from his hand at no more than a 20-degree slope.

"It looked more like eighty!" he said sheepishly.

"Now let your eyes look for other steep places, and for the most treacherous moguls. Notice each one carefully and rank them in the order of degree of difficulty."

John started to scrutinize the hillside, pointing out with relish the most difficult spots and telling me in detail what was so hard about them. After a few minutes he said, "Hey, I'm getting to know this mountain pretty well. I might become the world's greatest authority on Big Bumps someday."

"If you were going to ski this slope—and I'm not suggesting that you actually try it—where would you make your first turn?" I asked.

John looked it over and said, "Okay, I could make my first turn right there. Yeah. I could do that."

"And your second?"

"Yeah. Number two right there, and then there's . . . three . . . four . . . five . . ." His voice was calm as he concentrated on his imaginary run. Suddenly he turned to me with a smile and, without another word, pushed his poles into the snow and skied off.

Surprised at the suddenness of his decision, I followed, and was astonished at how much more relaxed and yet aggressive his skiing looked. He was off balance over a couple of moguls, but never really lost control.

At the bottom John was aglow. "Hey, that was fun!" he said. "I loved it. I might even get to like moguls!"

I knew that John felt good about making the run without falling, but I also recognized in his expression the greater sense of achievement that comes from having triumphed over fear.

John's victory was achieved by looking at the mogul field in detail and one mogul at a time. This objective observation shrank the imagined danger and, at the same time, made him aware of the realities of the situation: they were big moguls, but they were ones he could negotiate when unencumbered by fear. Just as in watching the seams of a tennis ball, the mind becomes calmer when it focuses on actual details, the smaller the better.

Speedophobia

Many skiers experience fear in direct proportion to the speed at which they are moving. Because they have often fallen when going fast, it is easy for them to associate speed with falling. To the extent that excessive speed is contributing to skiing out of control, there can in fact be the real presence of danger. Again the Fear 2 component is healthy and needs to be acknowledged and heeded. Self 1 can try to talk you into skiing faster than your ability to control yourself, either for the thrill or to prove to yourself or friends that you are not afraid. Again, fear in such circumstances is your friend, not an enemy. At the same time, there can be an illusory component of the fear of speed that disenables the skier who is not in any real danger. How to overcome this illusion?

When we ski, we are usually so conscious of trying to either increase or decrease speed that our perception of it is easily distorted. If we want to increase our awareness of speed, we can simply train ourselves to distinguish between its different levels, and to notice the relationship between these speeds and our control.

One way of doing this is to assign the number five to what appears to be your maximum speed and zero to standing still. Then as you ski, say aloud the numbers that you believe correspond to the speed at which you are traveling. As most people increase their awareness of these different speeds, they usually find that soon they are skiing comfortably even when moving at a rate that previously had seemed to threaten their control.

It should be noted that discrimination is necessary here. In other words, the speed that may be comfortable in easy conditions can cause you to lose control on more difficult terrain; moreover, it's virtually impossible to be aware of actual speed when you are far out of control. It is the relationship between these three factors—speed, terrain, and control—that is crucial.

Looking Out for Ice

One day during an Inner Skiing clinic, Tim fell while taking a lesson from Junior Bounous, the ski-school director at Snow Bird. When he had recovered, Junior asked him, "Do you know why you fell?"

"I have no idea," Tim replied. "Suddenly I just felt off balance, and down I went."

"Look over there," Junior said, pointing to a patch of snow glistening in the sunlight. The difference was barely distinguishable from the packed snow around it. "That's ice. You fell on that."

"Oh," said Tim. "I didn't notice it. I guess I'd better avoid that stuff."

"If you know how it affects your skis," said Junior, "you won't have to avoid it. Ice is more slippery than snow, so when your skis hit an ice patch, they tend to slide faster. Wanting to resist that downward slide, the skier usually leans uphill. Then his skis slide down further, and he ends up in the snow. But if, when your skis hit the ice . . ."

"Yes, if I'd gone with the slide instead of resisting it . . ."

"Right. Now let's go look for some more ice," said Junior.

Tim began looking forward to the challenge of skiing an icy section. What at first had seemed an obstacle to be avoided turned into something to be sought after, experienced, and enjoyed. Fear was decreased by curiosity, which led to increased awareness, which in turn reduced the unexpectedness of ice, thereby diminishing its danger. Soon Tim was skiing on ice with a remarkable degree of control.

Other Skiers

Sometimes the most dangerous hazard on a slope is above rather than below you—that is, other skiers. Falling down is frightening enough; being *knocked* down seems unfair. Again, increased awareness is our best safeguard. Before skiing a trail, notice the density of traffic on it, taking time to become aware of the degree of proficiency of the skiers and being especially alert to the presence of daredevils. Once in motion, we can develop an increased peripheral awareness of nearby skiers, just as players on a team learn to develop peripheral awareness of where their teammates and the opposition are.

What is recommended is *awareness*, not paranoia. If you submit to the fear of collision, you increase your chances of being hit, or at least of falling unnecessarily. If you become distracted by other skiers, who probably wouldn't have hit you in any case, you won't see moguls or subtle changes in the snow. In addition, you yourself become the danger you are trying to avoid. Although in rare circumstances a collision may be unavoidable, the way to minimize the possibility is the same as overcoming irrational fear of it: be aware and trust Self 2.

In summary, the illusionary aspect of a skier's fear of a danger can be decreased and even banished by increasing awareness of the slope itself. To do this, we must learn to overcome our tendencies to avoid looking at what we fear. We need to be willing to *know* the mogul, the ice, the speed, and the other skiers on the slope. This increased knowledge results in increased predictability, increased competence, and, consequently, decreased fear based on illusion.

If you find yourself experiencing Fear 1, allow yourself to look directly at those sights that seem frightening. Let yourself soak in all the details, one by one, of each obstacle. Look the dangers in the eye until you feel you *know* them—or at least until you feel you want to get to know them better. When you start to see obstacles as welcome challenges, fear will disappear. If you still believe that the slope is too difficult for you to ski safely after you have let yourself really examine it, then look for a somewhat lesser challenge. That's not cowardice but good sense. Remember that it's also possible to be deluded by Fear 1 into minimizing danger.

FEAR-LESSLY FOOLISH

We have all seen the Boomer, who comes down the slopes out of control. He has that look of mad determination on his face as he shoots down the hill, usually without turning at all, his body and face tense. Most of the time, he is wildly off balance, looking as if he's about to crash. Skiing beyond speeds within his control, he endangers not only himself but the skiers around him.

Such a skier may seem to have no fear, but what is more apparent is that he has little discrimination. Whereas the overly fearful skier exaggerates the danger of the mountain, the Boomer looks through the end of the telescope that reduces the apparent danger and thus inflates his perception of his competence. But perhaps the greatest distortion is his undervaluing of his own safety and of those around him. As a result, it is difficult for him to discriminate whether a particular slope is beyond or within his capabilities.

With bravado, the Boomers of life charge ahead into any situation. Trying to prove to friends that they are unafraid, they take foolish risks. Often they are attempting to cover self-doubt with a façade of fearlessness. In other cases, the Boomer is motivated by boredom with life and seeks situations of meaningless excitement to make it interesting.

Of course, there are real dangers to fear in the world, just as there are some slopes that in certain conditions are too steep for even the best skiers. One of the greatest problems Fear 1 presents is that in distracting us with unreal dangers, it prevents us from perceiving the real and present ones. With the world on the verge of a nuclear war, there would still be ski buffs worried about proper form on their turns.

A friend of mine returned from Hawaii amazed by the people of one town who lived on the side of a volcano that frequently smoked and rumbled but hadn't actually erupted for fifty years.

"They were just like us," he told me, "more concerned with the opinion of their neighbors than with the threat of the destruction of their town."

It is as important that we perceive real dangers as they are as it is that we see through illusionary ones. Accurate perception of peril prepares us to cope with it. Still, I have observed that in general people are more likely to indulge in Fear 1 when the actual danger is minimal. My mother was apt to panic if one of her children didn't arrive home when expected. Fantasies of an automobile accident would plague her, she would work herself up into a pronounced state of fear, and would try to alarm the rest of the family. On the other hand, when she found herself in an actual emergency, Mother was the calmest of us all; she knew exactly what to do and would take appropriate action quickly and with full mental presence. Fear 2 had replaced illusion-ridden Fear 1.

ACTUAL DANGERS

One may ask, "How do I know when the danger is real and I am feeling Fear 2 or when the danger is that of Self 1 and is simply in my mind?"

If you are in a state of physical and mental preparation (Fear 2), you probably won't even have to ask yourself this question, but if you do find yourself wondering, the best way to discern between the two fears is to notice your body's reactions. Though Fear 1 is born in the imagination, its physical symptoms have a strong sense of reality about them. We are definitely aware of the anxiety churning in the stomach, the shaking of the knees, the dryness in the mouth, and the shortness of breath. These physiological responses are no less real for being based on a magnification of danger.

It is simple to tell the difference between the tension and tightness of muscles caused by Fear 1 and the heart-pumping adrenaline rush of Fear 2. In Fear 2 there is a clarity of mind and an intensity of perceptions, while Fear 1 produces panic and unclear vision. Influenced by Fear 1, we usually are afraid to look at the trail closely because it evokes a higher anxiety, whereas Fear 2 enables us to see danger with a heightened sense of detail.

In most cases we experience a mixture of Fear 1 and Fear 2. There is usually some degree of danger present, along with the illusions based on

DISTIN- GUISHING BETWEEN FEAR 1 AND FEAR 2

Self 1's imagination. The goal is to decrease or eliminate the *illusionary* component of our fear. To the extent that we succeed, the Fear 2 that remains will increase our physical and psychological ability to meet the challenge at hand.

AWARE- NESS OF OUR ABILITIES

Once we can see the slope clearly, facing but not exaggerating its perils, the next step is to evaluate our competence to cope with the situation. It is this balance between the degree of difficulty and one's competence that determines the actual danger level of the slope.

We estimate our competence in several ways. The easiest way is through experience. Have we ever before skied a run this steep, this narrow, with moguls and ice? If not, how big a jump is this challenge beyond what we've handled before?

As we take our past experience into consideration, it's a good idea not to forget the specifics of the present situation. A run that might be manageable in the morning when you are most alert and fresh might be quite a different proposition at the end of a tiring day. Also, the trail that in the morning was cushioned with two inches of powder may by afternoon have hardened into crusty patches of ice that would make it a challenge even for skiers more advanced than you. If we trust Self 2, we don't have to think about such factors; we know intuitively. Self 2 knows what it can do. If it is given the chance to really see the slope, it will be able to assess whether the particular challenge is within its capabilities.

I usually trust the intuition of Self 2 in combination with objective observation and memory. I don't trust my thoughts—all those voices in my head that tell me, No, you can't handle that, or Don't be a coward—any dope could make it down there. Instead I ask my intuition, Do you really want to ski this or not? I don't try to persuade myself. I'm open to either answer. If I'm not sure, I look more closely at the hill and ask again, Is this a challenge I'm ready for, or am I taking a foolish risk?

From our experiences, we gradually learn what we can and cannot do. If we never accept challenges, we are left in the dark about all but our most superficial resources. But when our minds are freed from distorted concepts of our ability that are induced by fear, we can accept reasonable challenges without undue risk.

Self 2 knows the next step in one's progress as a skier. Self 1, on the other hand, asks, What will the others think of me if I don't take this run with them? If I can't keep up with them, they'll think I'm scared and won't want to ski with me any more. Or, Wait till I tell everyone I skied this run! Will they be impressed!

Self 1's urgings are related to the maintenance or aggrandizement of its image. Self 2's promptings come from our core and guide us gently toward realizing more of our potential. They seldom push us into an action; instead they lead us quietly, respecting our freedom to accept or postpone a given challenge.

I remember an occasion when Self 1 led me to take a very foolish risk. I was skiing with friends who were more advanced than I was, and they decided to venture through the woods into an unpatrolled area on the back face of the mountain. Something inside me told me that it was not a good idea. I didn't experience the usual symptoms of fear; I felt only a deep conviction that it was wrong for me. I was about to stop and tell my friends that I didn't want to ski this run when Self 1's voice chimed in, If you chicken out, they won't respect you or ski with you any more.

I wavered for a few minutes between that sense of knowing that I was making a mistake and Self 1's blackmail. When we reached the top of the back face, I decided that my first instincts were right. The slope was extremely steep with deep, heavy snow, and there were quite a few trees. But Self 1 came on stronger: You can't quit now! What will they think of you? Giving in to such urgings, I started off. It was a wild run, with many nasty falls—a thoroughly unpleasant experience—and at the end I counted myself lucky not to have been hurt.

Three days later I read in a newspaper that there had been an avalanche on this same slope and that three people had been killed.

DISPELLING
ILLUSION
ABOUT
OUR VUL-
NERABILITY

Though the most obvious vulnerability in skiing is the possibility of falling and suffering injury, most skiers are afraid of more than simply hurting their bodies. It is important to recognize that the fear of bruising one's ego, of damaging one's self-image by *failing*, is just as real. Recently when I asked a class of novices how many of them were experiencing fear, eight out of the twelve raised their hands. "Of those who are afraid, is your fear about falling or is it about making a fool of yourself?" I asked. Six of the eight admitted that they were as afraid of failing as they were of falling.

Another kind of fear comes from a less recognized vulnerability. It is what we might call "fear of flying": the fear of going beyond one's expectations, of letting go and relinquishing one's control to Self 2.

FEAR OF
FALLING,
FAILING,
AND
FLYING

The three kinds of fear—of falling, failing, and flying—stem from different vulnerabilities, and in order to overcome their negative effects it is useful to learn to distinguish between them.

Below is a partial list of fears mentioned by participants in a recent ski clinic, categorized by their particular vulnerability.

Fear of Falling

- I'm afraid of going too fast, of not being able to stop, of falling and hurting myself.
- I'm afraid of reinjuring my bad knee.
- Skiing is dangerous, and I'm afraid that if I get hurt I won't be able to go back to work. Even worse, I won't be able to ski again for a long time.
- I hate falling and getting cold and wet.

Fear of Failing

- I'm afraid I'll never learn to ski.
- If I give it everything I've got, and still don't do well, I'll know that I'm really no good. But if I hold back a little, I'll always have the excuse that I wasn't really trying hard.
- I'm afraid everyone will see how awkward and uncoordinated I am.
- I don't I look very good in these ski pants.
- I'm afraid of being embarrassed.

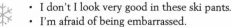

Fear of Flying

- I'm afraid of skiing too well because my friends will think I'm a show-off.
- I'm afraid of letting go of control over myself, even though I skied much better the few times I tried it.
- It's frightening to ski really well because then you have a reputation to live up to.
- When I really let go, it's as if part of me dies.

An effective way of increasing your awareness of vulnerability in general is to ask yourself some questions. What possible harm can come to me? Does the harm I fear threaten my body or my ego? Then be as specific as you can.

If you realize you're afraid of falling, don't stop there. Ask yourself what is likely to happen if you fall. In the particular situation, do you really think it is possible to hurt yourself seriously? Even if the answer is yes, what then? Is it the pain, the incapacitation, or the expense you fear? On the other hand, if you are only afraid that falling will make you cold and wet, follow that to its full conclusion as well. In short, neither exaggerate nor minimize the consequences of falling, failing, or flying.

I once asked a frightened skier what was the worst she imagined could happen. She answered that she wasn't as afraid of hurting herself as of not skiing as well as her friends.

"What would happen then?"

"Well, they might like me less, and not ask me to go skiing with them."

"Okay. And then?"

"Well, I might lose them as friends."

"And after that?"

"I guess I'd feel lonely . . . No, I'm sure I'd find more friends."

"And then?"

"They might even be better friends than the ones who would like me only if I skied well."

With little help from me, she had seen through her exaggerated vulnerability, and now her fear was gone.

Fear of Falling

Of course, the human body is vulnerable to injury when moving too fast to be able to control itself. We have discussed increasing one's awareness of the actual danger from the hill or from other skiers. Now let us examine how to increase awareness of one's vulnerability to being physically hurt.

Some people are more prone to injury than others, and so they experience more fear. For example, a ten-year-old girl in perfect health, with a little extra padding where it counts, is not as vulnerable as an older woman who has recently torn a ligament in her leg. If for some reason your body is particularly fragile because of a recent injury or some other structural weakness, it doesn't make sense to ski beyond your safety zone.

To think that you can't be hurt would be silly, but it's equally irrational—and more common—to exaggerate the probabilities of injury if you fall. Realism is gained by paying attention to experience—your own and that of others.

When you fall, try to notice what happens. There's no need to fall on purpose, but when and if you do fall, you can learn something from it. If you fall as a result of going too fast and allow yourself to experience the pain, you will probably be less inclined to go out of control the next time. If you find the fall didn't hurt as much as you thought it would, you learn that not all falls are painful, and your fear will decrease. This is often the case with beginners, who generally dread falling, and this usually causes them to tighten and sit back. But when they do fall, they find that it wasn't as bad as they had imagined. With their fear lessened, they relax more and hence fall less. I saw an example of this at exactly the opposite end of the spectrum—that is, the experts—while watching on television a special downhill race without turns designed to break speed records. To cut down resistance from the wind and snow, the racers used special equipment and reached speeds of up to 120 mph. On one of the runs a racer had a spectacular crash but was unharmed. In an interview afterward the skier said that the fall had actually made him more relaxed. Prior to the run he had been afraid of what might happen, and so was tight. After falling he realized that the worst wasn't so bad, and so wasn't as afraid on his next run.

In other words, whether novice or expert, it is important to learn by example; otherwise, experience has a habit of repeating itself until the inherent lesson is learned.

I once gave a ski lesson to a beginner, Charles, an Englishman who had been reading *The Inner Game of Tennis* and was enthusiastic about its approach. Whenever he fell, he would laugh and exclaim, "Nothing is good or bad. Falling is fine. Falling is fun!"

As I watched Charles I noticed that he seemed to fall whenever he was even slightly off balance. It was a cold day, and I grew tired of helping him put his skis back on every time he took a tumble. Finally, when he was sprawled out in the snow again, still blissfully smiling, I asked, "Tell me, how is it down there? Are you cold? How long does it take us to get your skis back on each time?"

Charles paused, assessed his body and his situation, and then said, "Actually, it's damned cold down here, and I'd rather be skiing than doing up my bindings all the time." Thereafter, he fell less.

Falling is falling—nothing more, nothing less. If it were more fun to fall than to stand up, few children would learn to walk. Falling is *supposed* to be a little uncomfortable; why pretend the discomfort isn't there? Painful falls teach us not to take unnecessary risks, define the extent of our vulnerability, and help us to make more intelligent choices.

Many skiers are more afraid of pain than of injury. The pain of a fall is real, but fear exaggerates it, often making it seem more intense than it actually is. Pain needs to be experienced as it *is* in order to avoid distortion. It is the body's way of telling us something; we need to attend to it rather than to ignore or to exaggerate it. Again the principle is the same: experience what is; be aware and learn.

MEMORIES OF PAST INJURIES

In my second winter of skiing, I took a bad fall and tore the ligaments in my right knee. It was quite painful. Even more painful was the ankle-to-groin cast that I had to wear for a month.

After the cast was removed, I exercised religiously until the leg was back to normal. That spring I played lacrosse, a physically demanding game that requires a lot of running, and that summer I was a lifeguard, swimming constantly in the ocean and running on the beach. My knee never bothered me; in fact, I don't believe I even thought about the injury.

But the first time I went skiing that winter a voice in my mind reminded me, "Better be careful. Your knee might not be strong enough, and you don't want to injure it again." I started hesitating a little, tightening up, favoring my right leg so that I wouldn't put all my weight down on it. As a result, I constantly fell when turning to my left.

Memories of past injuries enhance the power of Fear 1, telling us that the worst that has happened is about to happen again. Fear works by association. If we take a bad fall in a particular circumstance, the next time we're in a similar situation we're apt to experience fear. The present may be void of real danger, but the fear will still be there.

Memories are only memories. If we can keep our minds in the present, we will see the situation as it is and know how to respond. But if we let our minds project the past onto the future, we will see ghosts and tighten up, responding to the illusion instead of what is really there, thus increasing the likelihood of another injury.

OVER- COMING FEAR OF FAILURE

People, especially in our Western culture, are greatly concerned about not performing well enough to meet the expectations of self or others. It is not so much a fear of not accomplishing a given task or of attaining a certain standard, but of having the stigma of failure attached to one's self-image. It is Self 1's fear of losing face.

When I asked a young man who was worried that he would never graduate from a stem to a parallel turn what the worst thing was that could happen to him if he failed to improve, he answered, "Well, I'd never get off the beginners' slope."

"Would that be so bad?"

"Well, no, I don't really mind skiing the bunny trails. What would hurt is thinking that I'm a failure as a skier. I'd lose my self-esteem if I didn't get better."

So many of us have been conditioned for so long to measure our self-worth according to how we perform—especially at sports—that loss of self-esteem on the slopes seems a matter of importance. Identifying ourselves with our performance, we believe that we *are* how we ski. If we ski well, we feel that we are good, deserving of recognition, love, and respect. If we fail, we fear that we will lose the love and respect we need.

This belief that one's self-worth can be defined by success is implicit in the minds of many people, and I know of no way to overcome it other than by gradually seeing through the myth on which it is based. Human worth is *not* proportionate to human achievement. It simply cannot be measured in talent, position, age, wealth, roles, belongings, and trophies. Why not? Because the value of human life is beyond measure. At his core every person is invaluable and deserves all possible respect and love—not for anything that he or she has achieved, but simply by virtue of being human. The truth of this assertion is not easily acknowledged, but as one grows in self-awareness it will be gradually recognized.

Estelle was a middle-aged psychological counselor. After skiing for one morning, she was in tears and didn't want to continue. "I've simply never been able to learn anything in a group. Ever since high school I've failed at everything I tried to learn with other people around. I've achieved a lot of success, but it has always been with what I've picked up on my own. I really want to learn to ski, but I'm terrified because I know I'm going to fail again."

It was clear that Estelle wanted to realize two separate goals: to learn how to ski, and to overcome her lifelong intimidation in group-learning situations. I asked her which of the two she wanted more, and she answered that what she wanted most was to overcome her fear of failure in groups. "After all, if I wasn't so afraid, I'm sure I could learn to ski, and a lot of other things too."

Once this choice was made, all that was left for Estelle was to look failure in the eye and see just what it consisted of. We discussed in detail the worst that could happen if she failed to learn how to ski. "The last time you failed, where did it hurt? What real difference did it make? Did failing really mean that you were a failure? Who are you, anyway—someone who is worthwhile only when she succeeds, and unlovable when she fails?" Estelle edged closer to a recognition that she was neither her successes nor her failures, but the one person who was experiencing both. When she looked closely at the possibility of failing in the group ski lesson, she realized that it would be only a little embarrassing. She saw that failure was one experience, success another, and that both were simply experiences in the life of the experiencer, herself.

When we parted, Estelle was looking forward to skiing that afternoon. She had no idea whether she would succeed or fail, but somehow that wasn't the most important thing any more. What she *was* sure of was that she could learn and benefit from whatever happened. She was going to be alert and appreciate learning more about what failure or success really was. Already she seemed to be waking from the worst of her nightmare, and the decrease in Fear 1 could only make learning to ski easier.

In almost every case the key to overcoming fear of failure is a process of breaking one's attachment to results. Whenever we convince ourselves that results are all that count, we fall into an anxiety that paradoxically limits our ability to achieve those results. When the tennis player thinks he *has* to get his serve in because it's game point, tension takes over and fluidity and accuracy vanish. The same is true in skiing when we *have* to make a turn. The hardest thing in any achievement-oriented endeavor is to recognize that it is more important to stay fully present and aware than to strain for results. Our maximum potential is a by-product of awareness and of letting Self 2 express itself. Overconcern about achievement causes tightness and restriction of our bodies. The greatest competitors want to win, and hate to lose, but they aren't *afraid* to lose.

What is the value of learning a parallel turn if we neither enjoy ourselves nor learn something that can improve the quality of our life? Detachment from the god of success frees one from fear of failing, and then success comes much easier, for whatever it is worth.

Only Self 1 is vulnerable to lack of achievement; Self 2 neither benefits from success nor is hurt by failure. Children recognize this: they chant, "Sticks and stones can break my bones, but names can never harm me." The more we are able to recognize that failure is only a name and that we are not our Self 1, the less vulnerable and less fearful of failure we will be. The only real failure is not to recognize that you are more than your Self 1.

Fear of Flying

Self 1's third major vulnerability is its fear of achieving a state beyond its control by becoming totally involved in the present. During such a breakthrough experience, Self 1 becomes so absorbed in what's happening that it stops thinking, fearing, doubting, instructing, congratulating, or analyzing. Though this quieting of the mind helps our performance immeasurably because of the resulting increase in awareness, it is a kind of dying for Self 1. After the experience is over, it is always surprised: Wow, I don't believe it! Who was doing that skiing? How did it happen? Self 1 likes such skiing, of course, but not the fact that it occurred without any help from its voice. What would happen if the skier realized he didn't need Self 1—for skiing or anything else?

Self 1 experiences a dilemma whenever we start to perform near the level of our highest expectations. It wants the excellence, but not the loss of self. It is a hard choice, but usually Self 1 chooses its own existence at the cost of excellence. Tim often gives an example from the tennis court of what he calls the three-ball player. This is the person who, after the ball has gone over the net three times, says nervously to himself, Wow, this is a long rally. Of course, fear ends the rally shortly after the player becomes conscious of how well he is doing.

This same self-consciousness exists in skiers as they begin to surpass their expected levels, and it originates in Self 1's fear of flying. Having surrendered temporarily to Self 2's control and skiing "out of one's mind," Self 1 intrudes itself on the scene and sabotages the breakthrough run. Very few of us can experience a peak performance for long without Self 1's rushing in to admire, congratulate, take credit, or in some other way separate us from the experience. It's as if Self 1 is saying to Self 2, Okay, you've had your fun, but I'm not going to let you run the show any longer.

After the initial amazement and congratulations, Self 1 then generally attempts to repeat the breakthrough experience, but this time under its own control. It starts thinking about how it happened and tries to make it happen again: Gee, I was really skiing out of my head . . . that was beautiful . . . I think I must have really been letting go and being more aggressive . . . I'll just keep being aggressive . . . Okay, bend, weight, unweight, lean into it . . . attack. It isn't the same experience with all those thoughts and all that straining, but at least Self 1 feels comfortable now that the reins are in his hands again. It is programmed to sacrifice the beauty for the known sense of control, the excellent for the familiar.

There is probably nothing so challenging as changing one's means of self-control from Self 1 to Self 2. Learning new skills or new sports, or even learning to move in outer space, is nothing compared with the sense of the unknown when we change our way of controlling our bodies. Nothing is quite so beautiful as Self 2 action, and our dilemma is that we *know* this; we know it by the breakthrough moments when we left our minds and fell into the natural control of Self 2, the same self that produced the excellence and joys of our early childhood. To suddenly abandon Self 1 requires more courage than most of us have. But it is possible to do it gradually, and the more we come to trust Self 2, the more we lose our fear of flying.

Often when a skier is caught in Fear 1 he is so acutely conscious of his terror that it is difficult for him to focus attention on the slope. When the physiological symptoms of fear are overpowering, the skier often begins to be frightened of the fear itself: I know I can never ski a hill like this when I'm so petrified. At times like this, illusion can be decreased by focusing on the symptoms of the fear.

FEAR OF FEAR

A good example of the power of such awareness occurred during a program Tim and I were giving to a group of three hundred skiers. Wanting to make his point by example, Tim asked how many people would be afraid to come up on stage and face the audience. About a hundred people raised their hands. Then he asked, "Of those who would be afraid to come up, how many would do it anyway, if I requested it?" About two-thirds raised their hands. "Of those who feel they are too terrified to come up here, is there one or two who'd be willing to do it for the sake of an experiment?" Tim asked. One hesitating hand was raised, and Tim encouraged a young, slightly overweight woman to come forward. Once onstage she didn't face the audience, but stood sideways looking toward Tim, who asked her name and how she was feeling. "Barbara, and I'm scared to death!" she replied while blushing and giggling.

"Of what?" Tim asked.

"I don't know—all I know is I'm petrified." She was obviously more conscious of her fear than of the audience.

Tim asked, "How do you know you are afraid?"

Barbara looked surprised. "Because I feel it."

"Where are these feelings located in your body?"

"Well, my heart is pounding and my face is hot, but mostly I can feel my knees trembling."

"Are your knees shaking right now?" Tim asked.

"Yes."

"Does it hurt?"

"No, but I wish they'd calm down a bit."

"If shaking as much as they possibly could were measured as ten and not shaking at all was zero, how much are your knees shaking?"

"About nine," Barbara replied, but by now her voice was considerably more calm.

Tim asked if her heart was still pounding as hard and her face still as hot, then told her to focus her attention on her knees again.

"Huh, they're down to about five," said Barbara with surprise.

"All right," said Tim, "let's see what happens when you look out at the audience."

Barbara turned and stared blankly at the sea of faces. "Wow, the knees just shot back up to ten."

"Just keep looking out there and at the same time pay attention to your knees," Tim suggested.

Soon Barbara's knees were only at four or five, even though she was facing the audience.

"Where is the easiest place to look?" Tim asked.

Barbara stared at the back of the hall and reported that her knees were only at two. Then Tim asked her how far she could bring her eyes toward the front of the hall without an increase in the shaking. Her gaze came forward and stopped near the middle. "I can get about halfway," she said in a voice that indicated that she was becoming absorbed in the experiment.

"What do you see there that makes your knees shake?" Tim asked.

"Some people aren't smiling," Barbara answered, and started to laugh.

"Point to the people who aren't smiling," Tim suggested.

When she did, everyone started to laugh, and Barbara joined in.

"Look at the front four rows."

"Oops," she said. "Back up to a four."

"Look individually at the people in those seats," Tim suggested.

Some of them started to wave at her, and soon Barbara was laughing again. "I feel great," she said. "My fear is down to almost nothing."

Barbara stayed onstage while Tim continued his discussion of fear. Fear is like pain, he suggested; not something bad in itself, but an indication from the body that something is the matter. Fear 2 indicates that there is a real and present danger and the need for greater alertness, whereas Fear 1 signals the presence of an illusion about some unreal, imagined danger. But it, too, calls for a heightening of awareness—an indication to get out of one's concepts and return to what *is*. When recognized, both fears can be useful barometers.

There were questions from the audience, and finally one about the experiment with Barbara. Tim hesitated, as if thinking how best to answer the question, and then turned and asked Barbara to reply. Much to everybody's surprise, Barbara gave a fluent and articulate answer, with poise, calmness, and no hesitation. Without the interference of Fear 1 she had become a different person; in fact, the change was so striking that some people thought the demonstration had been planned in advance. But Barbara knew that it hadn't, and during the next break she came up to tell us that this had been one of the most important experiences of her life.

Awareness can focus on fear without fear. When we identify with fear we are afraid; when we identify with awareness we are that which is looking at the fear. This awareness is the part of us that is always calm, and it can be a helpful refuge when we are under attack by Fear 1.

As long as we identify with the parts of ourselves that change, inevitably we are subject to fear. To gain final freedom Socrates exhorted the individual to "know thyself." Castaneda's teacher, Don Juan, called those who attain this goal Men of Knowledge, pointing to the final destination of one who plays the Inner Game to win.

5❄

IMPROVING

For whatever reason they ski—fun, health, a chance to meet people—most skiers are disappointed if they haven't improved after a week on the slopes. The desire to ski faster and with more control on increasingly challenging runs is as natural as it is common.

All God's creatures have the desire to actualize their potential. A bird, for example, is born with the potential to fly, and its progress is simple and continuous. Improvement needs only some time, experience, and a little guidance from its parents. Without worrying about whether or not it is becoming more skillful, it manages to learn to soar on currents of air, to dive, turn, and glide. The bird's improvement is never in doubt; there is no strain, no forcing, no inferiority complex, no inflated ego—and amazingly enough, no lack of coordination.

Yet among human beings we see all of the above qualities, including lack of coordination, in their efforts to improve. Why is development so easy for the bird, and so difficult and frustrating for people? Why do humans try so hard to improve when improvement is so effortless for the rest of nature?

Fritz Perls, the father of Gestalt therapy, answered this question with the ironic insight that human beings are the only species of life that has the capability of interfering with its own growth. The human being tends to block this natural process by doubting his potential. He believes that if he can't do something right away it's because the potential isn't there. He concludes that improvement means *adding* something that he doesn't already have, *becoming* something that he isn't. "I'm not a good skier," he says to himself, "and to become one I'll have to acquire the necessary skills from somewhere outside of me."

In truth, what he needs to understand is that improvement is the natural process of helping something already inside himself to emerge. The oak exists within the acorn. The bird improving its flying technique is simply manifesting a potential inside itself from birth. To be sure, the acorn needs water, earth, and sun, and the bird needs guidance and experience, but the growth of each is a natural development of an already existing potential.

Although the distinction between these two approaches may seem obscure, the difference they make is startlingly clear. Improvement by allowing one's potential to emerge is unstrained, enjoyable, and remarkably steady. Improvement by trying to acquire an ability or quality that one assumes isn't there is usually frustrating and often halting. It is only because we employ our unique capability to impede our progress that we find improvement a problem at all, and this is why the road to improvement is often so difficult for the skier.

TWO KINDS OF IMPROVE- MENT

Because man interferes with his growth, his performance varies a great deal, often falling far below his capabilities. All athletes are confounded by their repeated tendency to perform brilliantly one day, only to fall apart the next. The level of a skier's performance at any given time is the difference between his present capabilities and the extent of Self 1's interference with them. He will ski below his actual ability in direct proportion to the extent of his mental interference. Free of Self 1 limitations, he will ski his best—that is, up to the limits of his potential as it has been developed to date. Further improvement will entail additional experiences to stimulate new growth.

Thus, there are really two kinds of improvement for humans. The first brings a person's skill closer to his present capabilities; the second is to learn new skills.

The remainder of this chapter will discuss the first kind of improvement: the ways of recognizing and overcoming the major obstacles that prevent us from skiing as well as we already can. The next chapter will discuss ways to facilitate the process of developing new skills.

In their desire to improve faster, many skiers overlook or neglect entirely the first kind of improvement. They think that they aren't progressing fast enough if they aren't learning or practicing something new. But this is not necessarily true; the mental interference that is keeping you from skiing your best right now will also make it more difficult to acquire new skills. Before replacing the dim lightbulb in your dusty attic, it makes sense to clean the bulb first to see how much light it gives off with the dust removed. Similarly, in skiing it makes sense to first clear away the doubts and fears of Self 1 that prevent you from shining your brightest.

Let's take the example of a skier who thinks of himself as awkward, and who has relatively little self-confidence in his ability. Because Self 1's beliefs affect one's actions, the skier's lack of confidence will be reflected in his performance. For instance, he may lean uphill, not bend his knees, and plant his poles stiffly and with bad timing because he is gripping them too tightly. If he sets out to correct each of these problems, it is apt to take him the better part of a season before these manifestations of his poor self-image are corrected. If he tries to change everything at once, his mind will become overloaded with multiple instructions and skiing becomes even more awkward. Yet if he takes each correction one at a time, he runs into other problems. If he decides to begin by leaning forward more, he is fearful because of lack of confidence, and so he has to force himself. This strain causes tightness and awkwardness. Even if he succeeds in making his body lean forward, his jaw is probably clenched with tension and his shoulders are even tighter than usual. In fact, he may even invent new postures to express his self-doubt. Trying to get the body to do what the mind doesn't want it to do is usually frustrating and time-consuming.

On the other hand, if the same skier is helped to overcome some of his self-doubt the errors that it is causing will begin to disappear spontaneously. Feeling more confident, he will find it easier to lean forward and to weight his outside ski in the turn; his shoulders, arms, and knees will be more relaxed and his pole plants will improve automatically. Eliminating only a single mental obstacle produces many physical improvements. As a result, the skier gains confidence in his ability, which in turn reduces resistance to absorbing new skills. Indeed, the skier may discover that what he thought was a new skill was already within his present capacity.

SELF-IMAGE AS AN OBSTACLE

Probably the greatest obstacles to growth of all kinds are our concepts about ourselves. By believing that I am not good at the sport, I limit how well I will let myself ski. Believing that I can't make good parallel turns, I usually won't. Nursing the idea that I am an intermediate skier, I delay the process of becoming an advanced one. These beliefs about ourselves are like the programs fed into a computer that, though it has the capacity to do many complicated tasks, can only perform within the limits of its program.

Self 2 is like an extremely sophisticated computer that receives an incredible amount of data from its experience, stores it in memory banks, and then uses it to refine movement and develop new skills. If you have a computer with the capacity to solve every conceivable square root, but program it only for numbers up to 100, it will not give you the answer if you ask for the square root of 1938. The limited programming doesn't cancel the computer's memory or mean that it lacks the capability; it simply prevents the use of its full potential.

Self 1 limits Self 2 in the same way. Its negative beliefs can't decrease Self 2's potential, but it can and does restrict its realization. Self 1 can't prevent Self 2 from being able to make a parallel turn if that skill is already within its capabilities, but it can keep the parallel turn from happening. Likewise, if Self 2 is continually being fed the idea that it is uncoordinated, to the extent that that programming is accepted, coordination is sabotaged. It is this tendency of Self 1 to impose limiting concepts on Self 2 that is the fundamental means by which man interferes with his own growth.

This is not to say that if you tell your Self 2 that it can ski expertly that it will allow you to do so. You can't program a computer to solve calculus problems simply by telling it that it is a great mathematician. This is the principal flaw of so-called positive thinking. Self 2 cannot accomplish tasks simply because you repeatedly tell it that it can; it will do so only with growth and experience, and when it has the necessary sensory data in its memory bank. Human computers can be programmed with positive or negative concepts, but neither of these alters Self 2's actual capacity. Telling yourself that you are an advanced skier when in fact you are a beginner is not going to make you an expert, and may even be dangerous. Rather than feeding in positive programs (which you may not even believe in) to replace negative ones (which you probably do), it is more effective to focus on eliminating any limiting concepts. It is extraordinary to see just how much a self-concept can interfere with one's ability to ski, and how much improvement will take place immediately after its removal.

I remember vividly an episode involving a woman in her late thirties named Harriet who joined one of my intermediate classes. Riding up in the chair, she complained of having been an intermediate skier for eight years; she was hoping that perhaps an Inner Skiing class could get her out of this rut.

My first impression of Harriet was of a woman who tried to please. She wore her makeup and clothes with an almost overconscientious attention to detail. Her voice was cheerful but almost inaudible and her language was as precise as her graying bangs. When she took her first run, I saw that her skiing fit her personality: she looked good and had no major flaws, but she was overly careful. Her turns were executed with a technique that reflected many hours of lessons conscientiously practiced, but they lacked rhythm, fluidity, and aggressiveness. Her movements looked deliberate and controlled, and she didn't allow herself to pick up the speed that the level of her technique seemed able to handle.

At the end of her first run Harriet shook her head self-critically, and I asked, "What's the matter?"

"Well, to tell you the truth, I don't know. I know that my form is okay. It should be. I've worked at it enough. But I'm really not satisfied. I'd like to be able to take more advanced runs, but I don't feel I'm good enough yet. I sometimes think I'm going to be an intermediate skier forever."

At this moment I used an Inner Game trick which often helps a student shed a limiting self-image. "Harriet, what kind of skiing would satisfy you?" I asked. "Can you give me an idea of how good you would really like to be?"

"Well, I think I'd like—"

"No, not in words. Show me," I interrupted. "Give me a visual image of what you want. Right now. Don't even think about it—just do it."

Harriet took off, skiing thirty yards down the intermediate slope in a manner very different from the way she handled her first run. A lot of her careful control disappeared, and in its place there was more spontaneity and power.

"Was that a little more how you'd like to be able to ski?" I asked when I joined her.

"Yes, something like that. I can't put my finger on what I was doing differently, but it certainly felt different. That was fun," she said excitedly.

"Your skiing looked more aggressive to me," I said noncommittally.

"Oh," she said, looking embarrassed. "Well, maybe, but I'm really not the aggressive type."

"Would you be willing to show me how you'd ski if you were?"

Harriet hesitated a moment and then skied downhill another fifty yards, amazing me and the rest of the class. Instead of taking her usual long traverses between turns she headed directly down the fall line, linking short crisp turns and picking up speed; she was attacking the slope, driving her knees and edging sharply. To be sure, she lost a measure of refinement as she poled vigorously and leaned forward, abandoning all caution, but considering the degree of difficulty of the terrain her skiing showed remarkable improvement.

"Is that what aggressive skiing would be?" I asked.

"I didn't think I had that in me," she exclaimed, apparently overwhelmed by the experience. "I loved it, but I doubt if I could keep it up. It's really not like me."

I could see that Harriet was confronting a common Inner Game dilemma. Should she believe the image she held of herself or what she had just experienced? Could this single example of aggressiveness replace a whole lifetime of trying to please others? "Can I be aggressive in the future? Why haven't I let myself ski this way before?" she might have wondered. It was not an easy choice to make: the safety of her old, carefully circumscribed self-image against the risk of her expanded sense of self. She had to choose between improvement and shedding a self-image.

What stunned the group was how improved Harriet's skiing had become almost instantly. She hadn't been given a single technical instruction, yet technical changes in her skiing occurred along with greater fluidity and rhythm. It was obvious that the ability to ski so well had been inside Harriet the whole time. What had released her potential was that she had ignored—perhaps only temporarily—the self-image that had been restricting her. In thinking of herself as unaggressive, she had skied unaggressively; but since she had never programmed herself to think that she couldn't "show" someone what aggressive skiing was like, she was able to do it, and skied much closer to her.

The next day Harriet reported triumphantly that for the first time in her life she had skied an advanced run—a challenge that had been within her technical competence for a long time—and had enjoyed it enormously.

What are the beliefs that you have about your skiing? Some of the more common ones are: "I'm not well coordinated"; "I'm not aggressive enough"; "I can't ski the fall line, take moguls, make parallel turns"; "I am a beginner." Now think for a moment. Have you ever had an experience that refutes that belief? If you are like most skiers I've known, you've had a run, or at least a few turns, in which your performance contradicted your self-image.

Do you believe your experience—which has shown you that you are capable of more—or your self-image? One way of resolving the contradiction is to chalk off the good experience to luck or fate or newly sharp-

80

ened edges. This prevents you from setting yourself up for disappointment and frustration, but it also keeps you from improving. The frightening alternative is to realize that there is more potential inside you than you ever realized, and that the real challenge is to shed whatever is keeping your potential from developing.

The tendency to form constricting self-concepts is so common that most of the time we don't even know we are doing it. The process can start innocently enough by identifying with our performance. Take John, who is eager to ski well and is about to take his first run of the day. In the past he has had both good days and bad, but being uncertain of himself, he's anxious about what will happen today. If his first few turns are a bit awkward, he may say to himself, This looks like a bad run. Sure enough, it is, and by the time he reaches the bottom he has convinced himself that the whole day will be a washout. After another run he notices that he is rotating his upper body as he turns—an error he'd thought he'd corrected last season; now he thinks, "I have lousy form. I hope no one's watching me." A few discouraging falls later, his dominant thought is, I can't ski moguls to save my life. Finally in despair, he reaches the conclusion that he is a bad skier and that he ought to give up the sport.

In a matter of minutes, John has increasingly defined and limited himself by his beliefs that (1) he is going to gave a bad run and a bad day; (2) he has lousy form; (3) he can't ski moguls; and (4) he will never be a good skier.

After programming himself for a day of poor skiing, John has begun a process that progressively programs a poor self-image. By thinking that he has bad form he identifies with a *possession*—his form. By using the word "can't," he limits his potential. "Can" and "can't" are among the most powerful words we use to define ourselves. His most limiting concepts are those thoughts that start with "I am" and "I am not." Once he believes he is a bad skier, he won't allow himself to have good form, be able to ski moguls, or be the skier he potentially is.

Self 1's image forming can go so far as to shape one's very sense of identity. At the end of a few days of unsatisfactory skiing, he may conclude that not only is he a bad skier but he is uncoordinated in general. After a few frustrating days back at the office he may extend the program to include all activities, and tell himself that he is incompetent. From there it is only a short step to "I'm no good at all."

How could John have stopped himself from forming these negative self-concepts? Not by trying to generate a positive self-image, but *by forming no self-image at all*. Having made three awkward turns, he could simply have observed to himself, Hey, those turns felt pretty awkward; this would have been simply an accurate description of a past event. When he fell on a mogul, if he had thought, Well, I haven't skied a mogul well yet today, instead of believing that he couldn't ski them at all, he would leave open, and perhaps even encourage, the possibility of improvement.

Does John gain anything by believing he's going to have a bad day and that he's an inferior skier? He gains a sense of security by predicting what is going to happen, thus preventing possible disappointment. At least at the end of the day he can say, "Well, I knew I wasn't going to have a good day." Or if someone sees him fall, he defends himself against embarrassment by thinking, Yeah, I know I'm lousy—so what? At the expense of improvement he gains a sense of comforting predictability about the future and about himself.

John's mistake is shared by many of us in our culture: we tend to identify ourselves with how we perform. If I ski badly I tend to feel badly about myself and to believe that I am less worthy of respect. On the other hand, if I ski well I feel good about myself, and therefore am convinced that I myself am worthy of respect and approval. I try to prove myself by improving my skiing. Self 1's concern with establishing a worthwhile identity for itself leads most of us into "the proving game." Being an exercise that focuses wholly on self-image, it distracts us from and inhibits our natural process of improvement.

THE PROVING GAME

An observant woman, Lynne Kaufman, who attended a five-day Inner Game residential workshop, described in an article for *California Living* the importance the proving game has for some players:

> I find my way to the condominium, Pelican 19, in time for lunch; the large living room is furnished with six round tables, the curtains drawn to an expansive view of sandpipers, cormorants and gulls. The other twenty workshop members straggle in. . . . most in their thirties and forties, Californians, fit, tan, professionals. Some verbal sparring at lunch: who are you, what do you do, who do you know, where have you been? Soon we will all be undergoing the tennis player's acid test—"Want to hit some?" and within ten strokes we will each have the definitive answer to life's supreme question—HOW GOOD ARE YOU?

Tim described his early involvement with the proving game when he was a ten-year-old tennis player. "I used to get up at six-forty-five on a summer morning, dress, make and eat breakfast (scrambled eggs and fried hot dogs) in six minutes flat, run a mile and a half down a hill to the Pebble Beach gatehouse, and then either hitchhike or run the remaining three miles to the tennis courts. Arriving at least an hour before anyone else, I would practice forehands and backhands against the green wooden backboard, 1041, 1042, 1043, 1044, etc., ad nauseam.

"When players finally arrived, I would play with anyone who was willing, not leaving until dark after at least twelve or fifteen sets, a lot of drilling under my belt, and half an inch of rubber worn off my tennis shoes. If you asked me why was I practicing so hard, or whether I was having fun, I probably would have been surprised. Sure, it was fun when I was playing well, but I wasn't doing it for fun. I was doing it to *get good*. I didn't know why it was so important for me to get good. It took thirty years for me to find out that the 'good' I was trying to 'get' I already *was*."

For most people the proving game starts with a definite but often unrecognized sense of "not being good enough the way I am." The basic idea of the game is to earn respect and admiration from yourself and others by learning to do something well. "I may be homely, but I'll show them! Wait till they see how many A's I get. That will prove my worth." Or, "They all think I'm just an uncoordinated brain. I'll take up skiing, practice hard, and become a really good skier. Then they'll accept me."

The essential point about the proving game is that it is usually played to substantiate something that in our heart we doubt is true. Fred sets out to ski more aggressively, takes more risks, and becomes a macho skier in order to prove that he's a "real man"—which he must doubt if he has to verify it. In general, players of the proving game tend to doubt their intrinsic self-worth, and spend their lives trying to demonstrate the opposite of their basic self-image.

Trying Too Hard — THE WEAKNESSES OF THE PROVING GAME

Provers always strain because the proving game begins in self-doubt, and trying is precisely the kind of effort that results from doubt. When a skier believes that he can make a parallel turn, he doesn't try, he just does it. We don't *try* to sit down; we simply do so. Trying is the overcompensation of a mind that doubts you can do something, and it almost invariably leads to the tightening of too many muscles, the most common single cause of error in sport. It takes effort to ski down a slope and make turns, but it doesn't take trying. Trying employs unnecessary muscles (we might call them "trying muscles") that inevitably restrict fluidity and cause a tension and awkwardness that hinder our performance. A well-known track coach says that tight fists and a clenched jaw are the sure signs of a slow time. He gets the best results from his athletes by asking them to run at four-fifths speed instead of all-out.

"Not trying" requires a trust in Self 2's potential, the essential ingredient missing from the proving game.

Here Comes the Judge

The proving game necessarily involves the selection of one or more judges who will approve or disapprove of me and my skiing. Often we end up paying more attention to them than to our performance on the mountain, thereby losing touch with the subtle feedback necessary to improve. As a result, my skiing plateaus and the approval I seek become more difficult to achieve.

Most players of the proving game start out seeking only the approval of their parents, but soon the list includes friends, teachers, coaches, and almost everyone on the slope. The more people I let sit in judgment over me, the more I have to live up to conflicting standards of right and wrong. When I give authority to others to judge my worth, I am at their mercy—much like the gladiators whose very lives depended upon the whim of the emperor.

Frequently the most merciless of emperors is my own Self 1, whose favorite role is to sit in judgment over me and everything I do. Who gives me the authority to judge even myself?

No Win

Trying to win the proving game is an endless endeavor. As one goal is reached another presents itself. First I had to make my high school swimming team, but the status of my varsity jacket wore out before the jacket did, so I had to earn a city championship trophy. Even a mantle covered with trophies, plus making all-American, didn't satisfy me for long, or prove what I wanted to. Doing well only led me deeper and deeper into the game. I doubted whether even the national championships or the Olympics would do it. Perhaps the answer lay in proving myself in a career—seeing how much money I could make—in the way I dressed or the company I kept and so forth. But the game was never-ending; there was always further to go to reach the top of one ladder, and then I was confronted with any number of other ladders to climb.

A basic law of nature is that the exterior is a reflection of the interior, and this is the primary reason that it is impossible to ever really win the proving game. We can't better ourselves by polishing our exterior image.

Because the proving game is founded on a false premise that "I *am* my performance," the only way to win the game is to stop playing it. How can you do so? First, by recognizing that you are playing it, and then by realizing that it is not the game you want to play. You begin to question yourself: Why is my image so important? Why do I feel badly about myself when I ski poorly, and glow when someone tells me that they think I'm terrific at it? Does my satisfaction come from believing that I'm a good skier and being recognized as such by others, or does it come from actually skiing well?

These two satisfactions are quite different. The first is Self 1's taking pleasure in a self-image and leads us into the proving game. The second comes from experience, and guides us toward the discovery game, in which the skier seeks to experience his potential rather than to prove it.

THE DISCOVERY GAME

In skiing this simply means exploring one's already existing potential to improve. Instead of trying to confirm something about myself by the way I ski, or to predict how I'm going to ski my next run, I let go of expectations and concepts and see what happens. My aim is to experience my skiing fully, to be as conscious as possible of body movement, skis, snow, rhythm, and balance. If I have a breakthrough run, I enjoy it, but I neither expect that I will ski that well on the next run nor that I won't. Similarly, if I have a run that I know is less than my best, I don't form a judgment about myself or my skiing; I allow the past to stay in the past and leave the future open. I recognize that abandoning my concepts may cause uncertainty, but I accept this small discomfort for the thrill of continually being surprised by ever-fresh experiences. The point of the discovery game is not to find out how *good* you are, but to experience your potential as it continues to reveal itself. Unlike many provers, the player of the discovery game doesn't aim to ski beyond his potential; he is simply intent on breaking through the mental limits he has placed on it. He doesn't wish to be more than he is; he only wants to allow what is already there to manifest.

There is little more to be said about the discovery game, since each person has to decide in which areas he wishes to explore his potential, and then set out on that quest for himself.

Below are a few "unsticking" games that we've found useful to facilitate the transition from proving to improving.

SKIING AS YOU ARE

At the top of the slope, resist any inclination to *try* anything. Don't try to ski well or badly; don't try to relax or concentrate; don't try to let go. Simply trust and be aware. In fact, don't let any inner- or outer-game concept guide you; merely ski as you are and see what happens. It's very likely that if you let go of trying, your skiing will be better than usual, but don't form any conclusions about *how* it was better or what you must do to make sure it stays better. Don't attempt to ski the same way or improve on your first run. *Accept what happens.*

Continue this process until you feel you have given up making a conscious effort. The point of the game is to experience your skiing as it really is, without the "help" of Self 1.

SKIING IGNORANT

A corollary of skiing as you are is a game whose only rule is to forget everything you think you know about skiing.

"How can I forget what I know?" demanded an irritated trial lawyer from New York.

"You can't," I replied, "but go ahead anyway. Erase as much as you can and see what happens. Don't think about how to make a turn, or whether you're doing it right."

"Wow! I don't believe it!" the lawyer said when he came to a stop at the bottom. "I skied just as well as when I was telling myself what to do."

"You looked better to me."

"I admit it was more enjoyable, but you can't expect me to believe that ignorance is the key to success."

"You were right the first time," I replied. "You can't forget what you know, but you can forget what you think you know—that is, concepts, images, and beliefs. When you do, all that's left is what you *really* know. Maybe that's a more appropriate way of putting it: only know what you know."

FUN

Ski in such a way as to maximize the fun of the sport. Forget all the do's and don'ts and ski for pure enjoyment. Don't assume that the way you enjoy your first few runs is going to remain constant. Go beyond your concepts of what you *think* will be fun; focus on what is really fun for *you*. Give your body permission to behave in any way that it wants; let it play while you experience the pleasure of it. Increasing your speed may be fun, or perhaps decreasing it, or alternating the two—first a greater challenge, then a lesser one. Or focusing on fluidity and grace. Or being deliberately awkward or being aggressive may be fun for a while. Fun may even result from experimenting with how to increase your edge control.

After playing this game for a while, ask yourself whether the fun occurs more during the moments of action or after you or others have decided whether the action was good or bad. Does fun lie in the experience or in the afterthought?

STUDENT TEACHER

As stated before, most of us are unaware of the extent to which we limit ourselves by the roles we play. Once I suggested to Julia, a high school student who was an early-intermediate skier struggling with doubts, that she pretend she was the instructor teaching the class how to make a stem turn. She blushed, stood stock-still for a moment, and then came out in front of the class. She began hesitantly, repeating what she'd heard about the rudiments of the turn, but soon seemed to lose herself in the role. She stopped trying to explain and demonstrated a couple of nearly picture-perfect turns. "That's how it should be done," she said coolly as we looked on amazed at the change in her skiing and self-assurance.

At first Julia was surprised, then almost embarrassed, by her new proficiency. "Gee, I never turned that well before," she said, and then, "How did you do that? That was a dirty trick."

"I didn't do it; you did. For a moment you became a part of yourself that can already do what another part of you says you can't. How did it feel to be the teacher?"

By perceiving the difference between our roles and who we really are, we can vastly extend the range of possibilities for ourselves.

DO IT

Many skiers have had the experience of skiing behind an instructor and performing better than usual, often taking runs they never would attempt by themselves. It's not that the instructor has taught them something new, but that they trust him, and so Self 1 stops worrying and planning and giving instructions. Our abilities on these runs are an indication of how well we can ski when there is no Self 1 interference.

Recently, I was skiing with Diane, a nurse in her late twenties who had been on skis only three or four times. She was putting a lot of extra effort into her skiing, traversing from one side of the slope to the other, then making a 180-degree snowplow turn to traverse in the opposite direction. There wasn't much speed at the end of each traverse, so she had to push herself arduously through each turn. Knowing that she would have an easier time by following the fall line more closely, I yelled "Turn!" as she was halfway out of her first turn. She did so, and then another and another at my instruction. After five turns she stopped and said excitedly, "Wow! That was fun! I didn't think I could do that!"

"So how come you could?"

"Well, I trusted you. I knew that you wouldn't tell me to do something I couldn't, so I had no doubts."

"And I trusted *you*," I said. "I wouldn't have told you to turn if I hadn't known you could do it."

Diane's self-image had prevented her from having faith in herself. In trusting me, however, she actually was displaying some confidence in herself. Many skiers need the encouragement of an instructor or authority figure who believes in their potential more than they themselves do. But it is important that this trust be converted into self-trust by the student; otherwise he is left with the feeling that he can ski well only when the instructor is present. Such people don't seem to realize that it was *they* who skied the run, not the instructor.

EXPRESS-ING QUALITIES

Identifying with Self 1 often causes us to focus on the existence of one quality or another in our self-image to the exclusion of others. For example, if I consider myself cautious, I will not believe that I am adventurous. If I think that I am an aggressive skier, I probably won't see myself as one who allows the terrain to guide me. But the fact is that each of us has the capacity to express all qualities. We can be assertive and receptive, cautious and adventurous, calm and explosive. However, because we have stressed certain qualities in ourselves, these are more developed than others; they are giant oaks, while the others are still acorns. By believing that the acorn is not there—that we have no capacity for receptivity, for example—we tend to neglect it and to rely on what we are more familiar with. Thus any development of this quality is stunted.

The goal is not to stress one quality or another; it is to know that you are more than all of them combined, and to be able to choose which to express at different times. Achieving a harmony within all our qualities helps us to express who we are. The Chinese call it a balance of yin and yang—feminine and masculine, receptive and aggressive, soft and hard. The person who recognizes and develops all his qualities can express each of them according to opportunities offered by different circumstances.

Those who play the discovery game usually find that exploring the individual capabilities and talents of Self 2 is more enjoyable than the proving game of Self 1—and much more conducive to growth. But is it, too, just a game? What do we really win even if we succeed in skiing up to our potential? We win the enjoyment of the experience and the satisfaction of performing at our best, but is this enough to satisfy us? And if we don't succeed in skiing our best, have we really failed?

Earlier in this chapter, it was pointed out that the desire for improvement is natural, that man has a unique tendency to interfere with his own development, and that the primary means of interference is the forming of limiting images about himself, and of trying to prove his worth. Our universal tendency to create self-images has made me curious about why we do it. Why are we so eager to accept beliefs about who we are, to identify with our performance, appearance, and roles? Why is my self-image and the approval of others so important to me? Why do I need "self-respect" to prove to others that I am worthy of respect? Do other creatures have to prove their worth? Does a baby? Since I need to prove my worth only to the extent that I don't know it, I am left with only one possible answer to these questions. I don't know who I am! Not knowing, how can I know my value?

What is even more interesting is the realization that *I must really want to know who I am.* Why else would I spend so much time and energy trying to identify myself with so many superficial externals? Perhaps that's the beginning of the journey toward self-knowledge. I am he who wants to know who he is. I am distinct from the other organisms of the world in that not knowing who I am and where I'm going makes me uncomfortable.

6❄
LEARNING
NEW
SKILLS

F ew skiers want to spend more time than necessary learning something new. Having only a limited amount of time on the mountain, they sometimes become impatient when awareness techniques are used in an Inner Skiing lesson to help them develop a new skill. Often they feel that they are wasting their time if they are not getting a tip or technical correction, since this is the way they have been taught in the past, and believe that it is the most direct route to immediate improvement.

The truth is that the more awareness you can bring to the practice of a new skill, the more easily, quickly, and thoroughly you will learn it. Our experience with Inner Skiing has shown that by focusing attention on each step the body discovers the best way of executing it.

PETER

Peter, a shy thirteen-year-old, was an intermediate who had been skiing for three or four years and loved the sport. At the top of a run I suggested that we first take some warm-up turns.

I noticed that Peter stood stiffly on his skis and even sat back slightly as he went into a turn. As a result, his skis were moving out from under him and he didn't have enough edge control. He was also overweighting his uphill ski. The total picture was of a skier who lacked real control and balance, but who got by on his quickness and natural athletic ability.

"Let's take a short run, and you tell me where you feel your weight is," I suggested.

"I feel pretty far back when I'm turning," Peter said after about ten turns.

"Let's work on that, then. Sit as far back as your boots let you. Feel that?" He nodded. "Let's call that a three. Move a little further forward, but with your weight still mostly on your heels. Okay, that's a two. Now stand on the flat of your foot with your weight equally distributed. That's a one. Any time you're on the balls of your feet only, that will be a zero."

After Peter had practiced feeling the difference between these positions, we took a few more turns. "Notice where your weight is moment by moment," I told him, "and call out the numbers during the turn. Don't try to decide where it *should* be; just feel what is happening."

 For ten more turns, Peter called out: "Three—two—three—four— Oops!—three—two—one—three—three—two—two—two—two. Gee," he said when we stopped, "I never realized how far back my weight was. I really felt off balance, as if I was always trying to catch up with my skis."

"Let's try it again. Remember, don't try to change what you're doing. Just notice it."

This time the first few numbers Peter called out were threes, but thereafter they were all ones or twos. He looked more on top of his skis and seemed to have more speed and control. "On those last few turns my weight was more on my whole foot. I felt more balanced, not so far behind," he observed.

"Good. This time I'd like you to do a couple of threes, then some twos, some ones, and even some zeros. Play back and forth between all the numbers."

After a dozen turns running through the numbers, we stopped and I asked Peter what he'd noticed. "It's hard to separate all the numbers, but one seemed to feel better than three. At zero I definitely felt that I could edge better, but it was a little scary, too."

I asked Peter to do the same exercise several more times without trying to decide what the "right" number was. "Just let your body do whatever it wants," I suggested.

Peter made a number of improved turns. His weight was forward more (mostly at one), his knees were in a deeper crouch, and his entire stance was more relaxed, but his inside ski was overweighted during his turns.

At the top of the next run I said, "We're going to try something different. It's called Russian Skiing. It goes like this: notice when your weight is on both skis and when it is on one. When it's on both, yell out, 'Twoski, twoski,' and when it's on one, shout 'Oneski, oneski.' "

On Peter's first few turns, he was "twoskiing"; gradually, however, he started weighting the outside ski as he went into the turn. It was inspiring to see how quickly his body had picked up this fundamental skill.

Peter was laughing when he reached me. "That was fun," he said, and then told me how much better he felt and how much more control he had when he had "oneskied."

"Do you remember which ski you weighted as you went into the turn?" I asked. Peter started to think about it, but I interrupted: "Let's find out. This time call out which ski your weight is on—right, left, or both."

A few turns later Peter said, "I noticed that I'm almost completely on my outside ski as I go into the turn."

We practiced this awareness exercise until Peter was weighting his outside ski consistently.

Next I drew an S-curve in the snow diagraming a turn. I marked the top as 12:00, halfway through as 3:00 and the bottom as 6:00, then asked Peter to notice at what point he shifted his weight to his outside ski.

12:00 1:00
       2:00
       3:00

6:00

After ten or twelve turns, Peter told me that generally he stepped onto his outside ski at about 2:00.

"This time I'd like you to take some turns shifting your weight at twelve, and some at three. Notice what happens and how they feel."

We went all the way down the slope doing this exercise, and at the bottom Peter said, "Wow! I have much more control at twelve."

We took one last run, during which Peter turned beautifully. At the end of the lesson he looked up shyly and said, "I've never felt so good about learning. My father is a racing coach and he's good, but everything always seems so hard. I'm the youngest in the family, and I always seem to make mistakes. But today there were no corrections; I only had to concentrate on what was happening. No pressure, a lot of fun, and my skiing seemed to improve automatically. Thank you."

"Thank yourself," I said. "You did it, not me. You allowed your body to teach you what it wanted to. I was just there to help you focus your attention. Your body's pretty smart, and if you keep tuning into it you'll find that you can trust it to lead you in the right direction and that learning can always be fun."

TIPS AND TEACHERS

After watching Peter ski, it would have been easy to tell him what he was doing wrong and offer some suggestions. Seeing that he was sitting back, I could have told him to bend his knees more and to move his weight forward. But such instructions would probably have distracted his awareness of the immediate experience and actually hampered his improvement. Had he started thinking about instructions, repeating them in his mind and worrying about whether or not he was following them correctly, the sensory feedback he received from his body would have been less clear.

Tips fly around a ski slope like snowflakes in a blizzard: "Lean forward on ice"; "Sit back on powder"; "Roll your ankles into the turn"; "Drive your knees into the hill"; "Weight the outside ski"; and so forth. But tips don't teach. Because tips are merely conceptual formulations, they don't necessarily reach the body with more than a general hint about what it needs to do. The body learns from its sensory experience and benefits from conceptual instructions only as a guide to a given experience. From its performance it picks up data that are much more complex and refined than any that verbal instruction could possibly convey. The proper weight shift depends on such variables as the steepness of the slope, the length of the skis, and the skier's level of expertise. The calculations necessary to cover all these variables would be too numerous and complex to set down on paper, much less to memorize.

As Self 2 accumulates nonverbal data from its experience, it organizes the information it acquires in such a way that precise muscle instructions are generated and our responses become increasingly efficient and automatic. Once you are into the experience, the tip that got you there can be discarded. The map that guides you to a specific mountain in Vermont isn't needed once you're there. The map is not the territory; the concept is not the experience.

If you were to trace one of those skiing tips back to its origin, inevitably you would find that it started as someone else's experience. Someone skiing moguls discovered that pressing down on the tops of them achieved certain results. He passed this on to others, and eventually it filtered down to you and me. Too often we use the tip to replace the experience, rather than letting it guide us into it.

Constantly repeating technical instructions to yourself is an insult to Self 2, which can remember amazingly complex body movements, whether or not they were ever conceptualized.

Just as a skier can easily make his gospel a series of tips rather than his experience, he can also become overly dependent on his instructor. A teacher who likes to demonstrate how much more he knows than his student often reinforces the pupil's self-doubt. If the implication is that you cannot learn without the teacher's instructions, the student loses any reliance on his own natural learning process because he will be dependent on an outside authority for approval and guidance.

Learning happens best when both instructor and student recognize that experience is the teacher. The role of the instructor is to guide the student into experiences appropriate to his stage of development. At the same time that the student is guided toward attentive appreciation of the sensations of his body in relation to the snow and his skis, the instructor is learning from him how to best lead him to the next step. If the instructor is simply repeating a routine pattern tailored to, say, beginners, he will miss subtle clues about the student's immediate experience and will not be able to guide him effectively. Eager to take the student on to the next step, to get him through a progression in record time, he may not notice an uncertainty about the last step, or even that the student is experiencing fear or resistance. Only the instructor who trusts Self 2 can be of help in the learning process.

HELPING CAN MAKE YOU HELPLESS

Often skiers reach a plateau at a certain point in their development. We can become stuck, for instance, somewhere between stem and parallel, and seem not to be able to get over that hurdle. We try everything—lessons, tips, instructional articles in ski magazines—but nothing seems to work.

Usually the cause of plateauing is an unconscious habit—a response to a certain situation that has become so ingrained that we no longer notice it. These habits can start when we are first learning to ski, but since they don't interfere with our initial progress, we remain unaware of them. Our bodies compensate for them, so that after a while they partially work. For example, a skier may be sitting back on her heels but be unaware of it because her body has compensated by shifting her trunk too far forward, doing double work to make up for the initial imbalance. When this posture has been held long enough, it comes to feel normal.

The key to breaking a habit is the same as for all natural learning: *increase your awareness.* In the darkness of unconsciousness habits persist—especially if we have prejudged them as bad, and blocked them so effectively that we don't even realize we have them. Hence, the first step in breaking a habit is to bring it into the light of your awareness. The second step is to do whatever you can to sharpen your focus on the specific

BREAKING HABITS

characteristics of the habit. Only then does the necessary control emerge to change the pattern.

Since awareness of habits is usually suppressed, an instructor can be helpful in directing our attention to them. I am particularly conscious of this because of a recent confrontation with some of my own habits. I was a beautiful ballroom skier. My skis were always together and I had great form on all intermediate slopes, and even on some expert slopes. Still, when I came to a really tough run with a lot of moguls, I would start to lose my balance and timing. I would also feel tightness in my thighs after a few runs, no matter what slope I was skiing. Knowing that something was wrong, I tried various techniques and exercises in order to pinpoint the problem, but nothing seemed to help.

Then one winter I took a lesson with Junior Bounous from Snow Bird. After I had made about fifteen turns, he said, "Bob, this time I'd like you to spread your skis as far apart as you can and take ten turns that way." I did so, but it seemed strange. I felt about two feet shorter, like a mad midget. In order to turn in that position, I had to lean over and weight my uphill ski much earlier. Nevertheless, as odd as this felt, I did notice that I seemed to have more control and balance even on difficult terrain.

Then Junior asked me to turn with my skis and legs as close together as possible. Since this was the way I usually skied, it felt more natural, but after a few minutes I noticed that something didn't seem right.

Junior asked me to switch back and forth several times between the two positions until we reached the bottom of the run. By then I had become aware of how forced my "ballroom" position was, and how much more tension there was in my thighs when my skis were kept together. Furthermore, my weight was often on the uphill ski as I came out of a difficult turn. As a result, my skis were sliding out from under me.

At the top of the next run Junior said, "Now follow me without thinking about your legs or skis," and took off before I had a chance to respond. We tackled some pretty steep terrain with a lot of moguls, and I was amazed by my balance and control. After a few turns I began to notice that my skis weren't as close together as they'd been previously, and that I was stepping into my uphill ski earlier and more emphatically. My legs felt loose and relaxed, and responded fluidly to the terrain.

When I reported this to Junior as we came to a breathless stop, he said, trying to hide a grin, "C'mon, don't think about it. Let's go. You're wasting time." And he took off again.

It was a breakthrough run. I felt so balanced that I couldn't have fallen if I'd wanted to.

 At another Inner Skiing clinic a few months later I joined a class led by Don Lemos from Aspen. Since my lesson with Junior my skiing had markedly improved, but I still felt that I was using too much effort, mostly in my upper body. After taking a run, Don said, "Bob, take a few turns as you normally do, but pay attention to how your head feels."

I did so, but was unaware of anything out of the ordinary. When Don asked what I'd felt, I replied, "Nothing," feeling silly and inspiring laughter from the rest of the class.

"Take a few more turns," Don persisted, "and see if you can tell whether your head is moving or if it's still."

My head felt just right—not too much movement, but not rigidly in place.

"Okay. Try a few more, but this time rock your head from side to side as much as you can whenever you turn."

This movement felt extremely awkward. Each time I rocked my head one way, I threw my body a little off balance, causing my skis to slide to the other side. But though it felt odd, I recognized something familiar in the motion. Then Don had me practice the other extreme—holding my head as still as possible during turns. I expected to feel stiff, but to my surprise I was much more balanced. We went through both variations a few more times, and soon I realized how much head rocking I had been doing before. At the end of the lesson when I took a run following Don's direction to forget everything I had just been doing, my body felt still and skiing became effortless.

Both Lemos and Bounous had used the technique of exaggeration to help me become more aware of my habits, and this helped to bring them into clearer focus.

Being instructed to exaggerate a "bad" habit also tends to relieve it of any negative connotations, and therefore makes it more accessible to awareness. If a student is told that he isn't bending his knees enough at the end of a turn, the criticism usually produces a resistance to focusing attention on them: thinking that not bending is "bad," he tries to change the habit before really being aware of what he's doing. Not knowing how little his knees bend to begin with, the student finds change difficult. But if he is told to see what it feels like to ski without bending his knees at all, he soon becomes aware of how ineffective this posture is, yet how similar to the way he had been holding himself, and he then begins to bend his knees by his own volition.

We all have habits. Some help us in reaching our goals, some don't matter, others are harmful. But any of them that are performed unconsciously detract from our overall sense of awareness of our lives. Unconscious habits put us to sleep and limit our alternatives; awareness awakens us to the range of our choices and potentials.

THE DIFFICULTY OF BELIEVING THAT AWARENESS IS SELF-CORRECTIVE

"There's got to be more to it than that," a skier says, finding it hard to realize that awareness alone can bring about changes in his technique.

Even though I have seen awareness work wonders time and time again, the phenomenon still amazes me. Like most of us, I had always been conditioned to believe that improvement results from telling oneself what is wrong or right, and then trying hard to stop the one and do the other. This belief blocks us from trusting the natural learning that takes place if we are open to allowing it. Even skiers who have improved initially without a lot of instructions think that there must be a gimmick, and look for a tip to cling to as insurance. Often they give the power to the instructor, believing they can ski well only when he's around, but the fact is that improvement occurs whenever *awareness* is present. The evidence mounts: trying fails; awareness cures.

To dispel my own sense of disbelief I began wondering *how* awareness cures, and the following analogy came to mind. Suppose you are skiing late in the afternoon. There is a heavy snowfall, reducing visibility of the slope to about 10 percent. Assume also that you are skiing under the influence of a general anesthetic which cuts down the feeling of your body to 10 percent. With so little feedback from the terrain and from your body, it would be virtually impossible to get down the slope safely, much less improve your technique. The body needs visual and kinesthetic information to make even the simplest adjustment. As we become more aware, the feedback is increased, and the body's ability to correct itself increases proportionately.

WHO NEEDS PRACTICE?

Often the removal of a mental obstacle or an increase in awareness leads to significant and almost instantaneous improvements. Something new and dramatic emerges. Doing something well once or twice shows the skier his potential; he sees that the talent and skill are actually there, and, of course, he's excited. But if this leads him to believe that practice is unnecessary, he is liable to be disappointed the next day when his new skill has vanished. We can't consider ourselves improved until we can rely on our newfound ability being there when we need it.

Practice often sounds too much like drudgery to someone brought up in a culture that believes in instant food, instant money, instant gratification. Everyone wants immediate results. We don't like to hear about how long it took to build Rome, or that enlightenment may take more than forty minutes a day. But the fact is that it takes time and practice to develop excellence in any endeavor. When a golfer or pitcher talks about "being in the groove," he is referring to a finely honed motion that took years to become ingrained. Just as cutting a groove in a piece of hard wood doesn't happen with one stroke, so learning to make a turn with ease on tricky terrain doesn't happen by doing it a few times. Self 2 needs repeated experience in order to refine its movements until an effective groove has been made.

But although I now realize that freedom and spontaneity come only from a lot of practice and self-discipline, I still believe in instant success. There is no reason why practice need be considered a form of torture that must be endured before the enjoyment of excellence is possible. Success can be had whenever awareness is fully present—at each step of the way, not just in reaching a final goal. It is because practice is so often regarded as something other than a truly experiential process that Self 1 gets bored so easily. After making twenty-five stem turns in a row, the mind tends to assume that it knows all about the maneuver; consequently we lose the attentiveness and curiosity that will make the twenty-sixth turn new and exciting. The succeeding turns are apt to be experienced through the dense fog of "Ho-hum, another stem turn." The ho-hum diminishes our receptivity; the bored mind skitters along the surface of the experience and is easily distracted because it doesn't perceive enough detail to hold its attention. When one is bored practicing, improvement is slow.

One way to overcome boredom is to learn to *play*. At a party I was introduced to a concert flutist, and eventually the talk turned to practice. "I never practice," he said. "I always play. I can play the scales for hours and have a marvelous time. I used to hate it when I was home practicing while everybody else was out having a good time. Then one day, instead of doing it by rote, I started experimenting with how hard I blew into the mouthpiece. I found that the sounds were different, depending on how hard or soft I blew, and this led me into listening to my breath as I played. I was delighted by all these subtle variations that I'd never heard before, and how I could control them. Now I can play scales every day for hours without being bored, and I never consider it practice any more."

One day I was teaching Ellen and Jean, sixteen-year-old twins from Texas who were very competitive with each other. They were full of enthusiasm and energy, always cutting each other off in midsentence. Intermediate skiers, they had just learned to step onto their outside ski to turn, but I felt they needed practice to groove their new skill.

When I took them to the top of an intermediate slope, Jean cried, "Hey, this is too easy! What a drag!"

"Yeah, let's hit an expert slope!" Ellen said.

It was easy to predict that the prospect of a half-hour's practice on weighting the outside ski would not be greeted by these two with much enthusiasm. Remembering my musician friend, I asked them to try something new. "If you don't like it, we'll take another run."

"We'll try anything once," they said warily.

"I want you to take a few turns and see if you can tell where in your body you feel the most pressure as you step on your outside ski in the turn. See how closely you can locate the exact spot."

Skiing down fifty yards, I stopped to watch. Rather than competing with each other or watching the teenage hotshots on the slope, their attention now seemed focused. When they reached me, they both started talking at once. "There was a lot of pressure right here above my right knee," Ellen began, but was interrupted by Jean. "First I felt my shin up against my boot, and then I started to feel the inside ball of my foot."

"All right. Let's see just how much pressure you have in these places," I said in an attempt to keep their interest level high. I explained the one-to-ten scale to them, and we took several runs, focusing on the parts of their bodies they had become aware of. While engrossed in these exercises, they were acquiring a lot of experience, and their weight shifts were becoming more refined.

At the top of the next run, Ellen said, "You know, I don't really like this numbers game much. It's too much like school. I have a better idea; let's call the scale rare, medium, and burnt."

We tried this for a couple of turns. Not to be outdone, Jean then chimed in. "Let's try colors. Red will be a lot of pressure, white medium, and blue only a little."

After this, they started using code words, points, even boys' names on one run. I had no idea what they were talking about, but once in a while I would shift the focus of the drill to edge control or some other exercise, and they would invent a new way of playing with it.

After four or five long runs, the twins' skiing had improved noticeably, so I asked them if they wanted to try a more difficult run.

"No, we're having too much fun here," Ellen replied.

"We'll catch you after lunch," Jean called as they raced for the chair.

CHALLENGING YOURSELF

Play is one of life's natural ways to avoid boredom. Challenge is another. Every skier has known the intense feeling of aliveness that comes when confronted with a trail slightly beyond his or her capabilities. This surge of sheer energy is our natural response to challenge; we "get up for it," as the saying goes, and often perform beyond our previous limits. Usually these peaks are reached when the challenge is not so far above our skill that fear or discouragement results, but is challenging enough to ensure attention. We can create appropriate challenges for ourselves during practice not only by attempting more difficult slopes, but also by reaching for higher levels of awareness and expertise. It can be just as satisfying to ski at relatively slow speeds tuning into the subtle body sensations—which indicate, for example, small but significant differences in degree of edging—as it is to race full speed through a mogul field.

An increasing number of professional and world-class athletes are using a mental skill called visualization to heighten concentration, refine skills, and prepare themselves for competition. It is said that before each game Jim Brown, the legendary All-Pro fullback for the Cleveland Browns, used his imagination to picture each play in which he would be involved and how he would react in it. Jean-Claude Killy and many other skiers have also used visualization the night before a race. Killy told a friend of mine that one night when he was practicing this he saw himself fall at one gate. Running through the inner movie again, he fell at the same gate. This time, however, he noticed that his line into the gate had been too extreme and so he had caught an edge. In his mind's eye he was able to correct the line and ski the gate perfectly. Taking the same line the next day, he won the race.

There is nothing mystical about visualization. It is simply the use of imagination and memory as a mental exercise. It is one way of practicing the best of the images that Self 2 has in its memory bank, thereby forming effective grooves. When visualizing a movement, it is most effective to see the image in as much detail as possible, and also to feel it kinesthetically. Experience what you would be feeling if you were actually skiing: your weight shifting as you make a turn, the wind in your face, your various muscles working. Hear the sound of your skis on the snow. Make your images as graphic as possible. When skiing is rehearsed in this way, many of the benefits of actual practice are approximated. Studies on visualization have shown that when a person sees in his mind's eye a physical activity, small but measurable amounts of contraction take place in the muscles associated with the maneuver, and that the same neurological pathways are excited by an imagined movement as by an actual one.

However, visualization cannot be a substitute for actual practice. It is only a supplement whose effectiveness depends on the depth of your awareness and ability to concentrate.

PRACTICE OFF THE SLOPES: SKIING IN YOUR MIND'S EYE

A SKILL WORTH PRACTICING

Practice requires motivation, and motivation requires recognition of the importance of the practice. Nobody will try to perfect a parallel turn unless skiing is important to him. Instead of regarding practice as the repetition of various physical exercises, the Inner Skier recognizes that he is also exercising important inner skills. Primarily he is disciplining the focus of his awareness or concentration. Some skiers use concentration to improve, but the Inner Skier places its value above the benefits it brings to his technique on the mountain. He recognizes that improvement in skiing will be useful only on the slopes, whereas concentration is a skill that is desirable in every human activity. For the Inner Skier it makes more sense to ski in order to increase his concentration than to concentrate in order to improve his skiing. Developing the art of concentration is probably the most practical and universally beneficial skill a human being can develop; it is the subject of Chapter 8.

7❄
DISCOVERING
SKIING
TECHNIQUE

In the teaching of sports there is a pendulum that swings between the fire of creativity and the form of doctrine. As in all creative processes, the fire needs some form and the form needs some fire. As Robert Frost said, poetry without meter is like playing tennis with the net down.

The same is true of learning and teaching any skill. The discovery of a better way of doing something happens in a breakthrough moment that cannot be easily anticipated or consciously controlled. Often it occurs at a subtle level without the person knowing that the learning is taking place. Most often it is in retrospect only that one looks back on a piece of performance and in surprise says, "How did I do that?"

If the athlete wants to repeat the superior performance or teach it to another, it is understandable that he seeks to put it into language that can be recalled and communicated. But once the body's movement has been put into the form of language, described either mechanistically or metaphorically, it enters a different domain. The movement that existed in the domain of direct experience has been transferred to the domain of language and concept. The question arises, how easy is it to go from the description back to the desired movement?

We would like to think that this process is easier than it is. Of course, it is easy if the movement is a simple one. If I say, "Raise your hand," you can do it without thinking. But if I say, "Raise your hand in such a way that the angle formed by your wrist gradually increases as your hand moves higher, and, at the same rate, close your fingers into a fist." This

107

movement is nowhere near as complex as a turn in skiing, but still quite difficult to transfer from language to action. If you are still not convinced, try to explain to someone who has never eaten a papaya how it tastes.

Language is not experience. Experience by its nature is complex, rich in texture, concrete, fleeting, individual, and, in great part, subjective. Language, on the other hand, is symbolic and abstract by nature and is greatly limited in its ability to represent experience. Muscles don't understand English or any man-made language. The language of *feel* is different than the language that attempts to capture it, no matter how artful the metaphor or how biomechanically accurate. Yet clearly, artfully formulated principles and technical instructions have great value to the student of skiing. The point is that these should be crafted with great consideration for the *learner* who has to use them to cross the chasm between language and action. It is not within the scope of this chapter to articulate all the instructions that might be necessary to develop the skills of skiing. Instead, I want to make a clear distinction between instructions that *command the body* and those that *direct the attention*. Then I will give examples of how to translate the technical instruction into an awareness instruction in a way that facilitates learning directly from experience.

By way of summary of earlier chapters, I hope the obvious is now clear—that increasing proficiency at any skill is a function of awareness, trust, and choice. Whatever interferes with any of these three functions will inhibit the process of learning. If one's self-confidence is undermined in the process of receiving instructions, the possibility for learning will be impaired. If, on top of this, there is pressure from the instructor to do it "by the book" or risk displeasing him, Self 1 has the opening to inject fear, doubt, and distraction into the learning environment. It is ironic how instructions designed to help the student so often do the opposite.

Listen to this instruction: "Initiate your turns from a place on your foot that is just in front of your heel and behind your arch." If the skier has not made this connection from his own experience, what is apt to take place in his or her mind when the instruction is given? Do we not tend to hear this kind of instruction from the same part of ourselves that was taught all the "right" ways of doing things at school? Probably none of us entirely escaped the conditioning that prescribes external models that are said to be "correct" and that expects students to conform. As a result, many of us have a love-hate relationship with such commands. We like them because they give us a sense of certainty and we are used to coping with them. On the other hand, we hate them because they put us in a position where our performance can be judged and we doubt whether we will succeed. The main problem with this approach is that the technique comes from the instructor's experience and not from the students'. The challenge is to benefit from the technical knowledge of others without undermining our own self-discovery process.

Now listen to the same lesson given as a *do* instruction: "Locate the point of pressure on your foot that initiates the turning of your ski." Do you hear any implication that you are doing anything "wrong" that needs to be corrected? No. It is an instruction to your attention, not a demand to change anything. In effect, it says, "Look over there. What do you notice?" Because you can't really give a wrong answer to this question, there is no fear of judgment induced in the skier. But if the skier does look, feel, or listen "there," something important to the learning process might be discovered. Noticing exactly where on your foot you feel the initiation of a turn will automatically help you then find the "feel" that works best for your body at your level of proficiency. In short, the instruction points you in a direction that enables you to *discover* technique. And this, I would say, is the purpose of all good instruction—to help the individual learn better and better technique from his or her own experience. Then if the student or the instructor wants to put language on what has been discovered, it can be done with some assurance that there will be more viable connections between the two. And these connections can help facilitate repeated access to the newly learned skill.

KNOWLEDGE AS GOAL; AWARENESS AS MEANS TO THE GOAL

The evolution of teaching over the last twenty years has reached the point where most instructors realize that their job is not so much to *teach* others what they know as it is to help the skier learn to do what he or she is ready to learn. This shift of premise focuses the attention less on fitting the student into a model for correct skiing and more on listening and watching for what is going on within the student's experience. The instructor becomes more and more interested in what the skier is experiencing than in whether or not proper form is happening at any given point. Why is it important to know what the skier is experiencing, especially if what is being experienced might be "wrong"? Because it is *through becoming more directly clearly aware of what is happening in the moment that the changes take place that later are called learning.*

The instructor can see what the skier's body is doing and can compare that with any model called "correct." But without asking, the instructor has no way of knowing what the skier is aware of during any set of movements. And this is the critical point in learning. When asked questions about balance, edging, pressure points, terrain, movement, rhythm, etc., the student automatically starts to become more and more attentive to the factors of experience that aid in the student's development.

So in this model, what is the role of the greater knowledge and experience that the instructor possesses? Once it is seen how even accurate knowledge can be a disservice to the learning process, it is easier to see how it can also be of great benefit. Theoretically, any skier who knew the basics of learning from experience is capable of learning everything necessary about skiing. But the learning could be greatly facilitated by a good and knowledgeable coach.

Such a coach would use technical knowledge in a different way than the traditional teacher. Understanding that no instruction can really capture the complexity of experience, he or she would not give instructions so much as *commands*, but more as *hints* about a desired outcome. A hint about a goal is a very different thing from a command to do something a certain way. It does not carry with it the implication of "right and wrong." Rather, it's a friendly clue designed to ease your discovery of something for yourself—as if to say, "You are going to learn to turn from your own experience and your turn will end up looking, feeling, something like this . . ." The lack of exactness in the instruction allows room for the individual skier to find his or her own way to what works, without feeling molded into someone else's model.

Pure exploration without a sense of what one is looking for can take a long time. The value of technical knowledge, when used as an approximate *goal*, is that it gives the student a sense of direction and focus. For example, it might take a student unnecessarily long to learn to weight the downhill ski instead of leaning back toward the hill as initial instinct dictates. A pure awareness instruction might be, "Notice how your weight is distributed between your uphill ski and your downhill ski." This instruction, with appropriate follow-up questions, would produce the desired result in time. But the goal might be reached more easily with the following set of instructions: "Placing more weight on the downhill ski than on the uphill ski will give you more balance and will make turning easier. What I want you to explore is how much more to weight it. You can try weighting different amounts and look for what feels best and what works best for you." In this case I am not worried about doing it right or doing it wrong, because I've been told to explore. At each step of the way I am paying attention to my own experience and am looking for *my* destination. My instructor observes my learning process and may make recommendations to see what happens if I increase or decrease the weight distribution. But these recommendations are not so much trying to get me to do it right as they are aiding my process of self-discovery. Because my primary reference is my own experience, I become more capable of knowing when I am on or off track. The instructor is thus playing the role of making me more and more independent.

Why should students be independent and in control when it comes to learning? Because each student *is* in control of the learning happening within him or her. The coach is there to *facilitate* that learning and should closely monitor the quality of the learning environment created for the student. In short, teaching should not be the primary focus of the teacher. The goal is learning. Artful facilitation of the development of skills and increasing the student's love and capacity to learn is not only of great value to the student but also has the potential to bring great joy to the coach.

LEARNING TO TRANSLATE TECHNICAL INSTRUCTIONS INTO AWARENESS INSTRUCTIONS

It is possible to gain the benefit of technical instructions, whether from an instructor or the printed page, without inviting Self 1 doubts and judgments into your head. It requires learning the skill of translating technical "do" instructions into awareness instructions. Using the above example, let's say you are given the instruction, "X percent of your weight should be on your downhill ski." You can safely assume that finding the optimal distribution of weight on the skis is important and worthy of your attention. You can decide to focus your attention on how your weight is distributed on your skis from the start of the turn to the finish. You can also assume that the desired outcome will be more weight on your downhill ski, thus giving you a narrower range of experience to explore. As you take your next turns, you start noticing how your weight shifts from one foot to the other, when, and how much. You do this without *trying* to change what you are currently doing, but *trusting* your Self 2 to move toward what feels and works best. Because you are in the observation mode instead of the achievement mode, you will get richer feedback from your experience and natural learning is inevitable. Even if your instructor or your Self 1 was to praise you for obeying and take credit for your improvement, you will know how the learning really happened and can distribute credit where credit is due.

Once you get the hang of it, it is not difficult to translate any technical instruction into a guided awareness instruction. Following is a table of a few common instructions given on the ski slope with examples of how they could be translated. In all cases the technical instruction is used to describe the desired direction, movement, or destination, while awareness and trust is your "focus of attention" as you move toward the best solution for you.

Target Area: BEGINNER "Straight run to wedge turn"—
First direction changes

Technical instruction	Focus of attention
As you glide downhill, push your right ski out so it points a bit to the left.	The direction of your right ski.
As you do so, tilt the ski you are pointing gently onto its edge.	The degree of edge of your right ski.
And gently press down on it until it carries you to the left.	The degree of pressure on your right ski.
Summary: Point the foot and ski, edge gently, and press down on it.	Direction, edge, and pressure on your right ski.

Target Area: INTERMEDIATE "Wide-track parallel"—
The pole plant

Technical instruction	Focus of attention
To strengthen our ability to ski steep terrain and to build in rhythm of turning let us begin working on the pole action:	
Go straight on this shallow hill and rhythmically plant alternately the right and left ski in this fashion (demonstration).	Listen to the cadence of your pole plants saying "right" or "left" the moment you hear/feel each plant. Do this until you find your rhythm.
Now begin to bow toward the pole each time you plant it.	The extent of bow at each plant.
Now push the ski tails to the side you plant the poles on.	Extent of pushing with knees. The angle of the tails of your skis.

Target Area: ADVANCED "Improving smooth linkage of turns by emphasizing angular movements"

Technical instruction	Focus of attention
Having practiced short radius, rhythmic turns, let us learn to ski with a quiet torso that is mostly facing downhill while the legs swing from side to side like a clock pendulum as we move from turn to turn.	Quietness and direction of torso. The cadence of your legs swinging from side to side. Say "right" or "left" at the beginning of each swing. How regular are the beats of the swings?
Let us ski rhythmically linked S-shaped turns by gradually daring ourselves to swing feet and skis farther and farther out from beneath torso and arms.	Gradually explore the range that your feet can swing outside of your torso and arms. Listen for changes in the cadence.
Let's further accentuate the movements we are practicing by prominently pressuring the outside ski of each turn.	Extent of pressure on the outside ski of each turn.
Rock fore and aft on your feet while standing still. During any turns of this nature you will feel yourself going through this rocking movement from balls to heel of the feet as the skis carve from side to side underneath your quiet torso. Now let's practice:	Notice what it feels like to rock fore and aft on your skis while standing. We will practice feeling that rocking movement from balls to heels of the feet while making turns. How quiet is your torso?
In turn entries, feel increased pressure on the balls of the feet.	The pressure on your feet at the entry.
In midpoints of turns, feel yourself pressuring the skis through mid foot.	The pressure on your feet at midturn.
In turn exits, feel the pressure rock toward the heels.	The pressure on your feet at exit.

113

Now let's practice turns where we notice all three phases smoothly linked together, fine-tuning our comfort with the balance play within the sweet spot range.

The pressure on your feet during the entire turn. Degree of comfort during entire play of balance within the sweet spot range.

Target Area: ADVANCED "Looking for the sweet spot"

Technical instruction	Focus of attention
As does other sports equipment, skis have a sweet spot. When you are balanced over the midpoint area of the foot, the skis will produce carved turns with great ease and powerful grip on the snow.	On what part of your foot are you balancing? Keep observing until you find the sweet spot, the place of balance that produces the greatest ease of turn and most powerful grip on the snow.
As we practice balancing over the sweet spot of the skis, we will realize that what we refer to as a spot is actually a wider underfoot "range," reaching from the balls of the feet to the heels. This becomes significant when we observe how that balancing point moves from the balls of the feet at the beginning of the turn to the midfoot range during the midpoint of the turn to the heels as we get closer to the exit of the turn.	Notice any movement in the sweet spot during the turn. Check where your balancing point is at the beginning of the turn compared to where it is at the exit of the turn. Do you notice any pattern in this movement?

8 ❄

RELAXED
CONCENTRATION:
THE MASTER
SKILL

T hroughout my youth it seems I was always being told to pay attention and not let my mind wander. This advice from coaches, teachers, and
parents usually came when I was performing poorly. If I struck out, there
was that familiar reminder to keep my eye on the ball; if I didn't know
the answer in class, I was told to stop dreaming. I would try hard to pay
attention, but somehow fantasizing about the girl with long braids in the
third row or about being a famous baseball star seemed more interesting
than learning the capital of Ecuador or the square root of 625.

Inevitably I would be sent down to the principal's office: "Young man,
you've got to learn to concentrate or you'll never amount to anything!"
But since I hadn't yet reached my teens, getting ahead in the world
wasn't as important as playing in the park with my friends, so I didn't pay
attention to him either.

Still, the message that concentration was necessary if I wanted to perform well did filter through my resistance. When I am having a bad run
skiing, for instance, I am aware that it is usually because my mind is not
focused on what I am doing. I know that if I don't pay attention I'm going
to have a disastrous day, so I tell myself that I have to concentrate. After
a while this becomes "Concentrate, damn it!" But this attempt to force
concentration results in a wrinkled brow, clenched jaw, tight shoulders
and arms. At this stage, focusing attention is difficult because I am concentrating on *trying to concentrate* rather than on my skiing. As a result, I
don't feel my body or skis or see the slopes clearly; I have substituted one
set of distractions for another, as well as increasing tension and tightness.

WHAT IS CONCEN-TRATION?

When concentration is painful, difficult, or strained, it is no longer concentration. Notice the absorption of children at play and you will see a beautiful example of what concentration is. The child's mind is relaxed but totally engaged. There is no thinking about the activity—just pure experiencing. The attention of the child is focused on everything he's doing, and though it may not stay long on a single object, it passes from one interest to another in an unbroken flow. Or watch a cat waiting in the grass for a gopher to emerge. Its attention is held steadily for long periods of time, its body poised, waiting for the moment of action. To remain steadily focused, does the cat have to tell itself, "I gotta concentrate, I gotta concentrate"? We can learn the simple lesson of relaxed concentration from small children and animals just as we did the natural learning process.

Human beings concentrate best when they're not trying hard to do so, but are simply interested in what's taking place. During an exciting movie the audience doesn't have to remind itself to watch the screen.

The simple law of concentration is that it follows interest. Where our interest is, our mind is. If the interest is strong, concentration will follow. If the interest is weak, attention will be easily distracted. We have to force concentration only when we are trying to focus on something we really are not interested in at that moment. When a person is somewhere he doesn't want to be, he does so in body only and lets his mind escape. We've all had the experience of talking to a person who is really a million miles away, even as he smiles and nods appropriately. Indeed, we have all been that person from time to time; we allot 10 percent of our attention to present circumstances; the other 90 percent is somewhere else.

The ability of the mind to flee the present is another unique capability of the human species. Or perhaps it is the same capability we use to interfere with our learning and growth. Babies and animals don't become lost in mind trips into the not-here and not-now. But the adult mind can all too easily escape the present reality and in an instant be anywhere else in the universe.

Earlier we compared awareness to light. Paying attention means focusing the light of awareness in order to see farther, deeper, or in greater detail in a particular direction. To pursue this analogy, concentration is similar to turning a 1,000-watt bulb shining equally in all directions into a beam of light that focuses on a target. When the diffused light becomes a beam, we no longer see the surroundings, but we greatly increase our awareness in the single direction the ray is shining. Concentration is simply the process of focusing the light of attention, of turning the beam into a laserlike ray.

When we lose attentiveness, the light energy of our awareness is diffused. We may have 1,000 watts to illuminate what is happening to our bodies and skis on the snow, but if part of our awareness is wasted in thinking about such future possibilities as how well we're going to ski this run, whether we might be hurt or the like, and another part is remembering past mistakes, and still a third part is thinking about the business or how things are back home, we will have very little awareness to devote to our skiing. In such circumstances it's easy to miss details of the terrain or the messages your body is sending you.

The Inner Skiing exercises mentioned in this book so far have been practical applications of the simple principle of relaxed concentration. But though the importance of a concentrated mind to achieve high levels of performance is well recognized, the need for it in the learning process is not sufficiently acknowledged. Learning is a simple function of memory. If Self 2 didn't automatically remember its skiing experiences, every run would be like your first. The images in Self 2's memory bank are essential to good skiing. What is in the memory bank of an expert skier? First, it obviously is packed with images, primarily visual and kinesthetic impressions. But good skiing is not simply the result of the *quantity* of images in the bank; their *quality* is what counts most. For example, if the skier is scared most of the time, the images he retains are going to be out of focus and therefore less useful. Likewise, if he is bored, and goes through repetitive movements without interest, he may accumulate a lot of dull images which lack enough vividness to stand out in sharp contrast. Skiing scared is like shaking the camera; skiing bored is like taking a picture without enough light. Neither produces the necessary clarity of image. On the other hand, if the camera is still and there is enough light on the scene, a clear picture will be stored from which Self 2 can extract accurate muscle instructions for the future. Self 2 can learn more from clear images of mistakes than from blurred, dull images of a good run. Excellent skiing results from a large number of high-quality images.

The enjoyment inherent in concentration also needs to be stressed. As a person can concentrate, so he can enjoy. Whenever we let our minds become truly absorbed in an activity, it is enjoyable. Even the most simple and unchallenging actions become a pleasure to perform when our attention is wholly present. Perhaps that's why children laugh so easily. When the mind is absorbed, it is quiet and doesn't want to wander. When restlessness disappears, we enjoy; conversely, when our minds are inattentive, we experience discomfort.

THE IMPORTANCE OF CONCENTRATION

WHO IS IN CONTROL OF YOUR ATTENTION?

Who or what chooses where our attention goes? Can you consciously decide to keep your attention on the present moment—on skiing, for instance—and have your mind happily obey? Or does it seem to have a will of its own? Often our attention seems to be a slave to the whim of the frequent and conflicting desires of Self 1. Who can order his mind to stop thinking and focus on the experience? Will your mind keep focused on the tennis ball, or the edges of your skis, or on this problem, or this book, for as long as you ask it to? Any of us can make such a request, but we seldom do, because we know that our minds probably won't obey, and then we would be confronted with the unpleasant fact that our attention is not under our control.

The practice of relaxed concentration is an attempt to regain a fundamental human freedom: the freedom to experience whatever in life we consider most satisfying, beautiful, and true. When we practice keeping our attention focused on the goal of our choice we begin to regain that freedom and the power that comes with it. To the extent that a person loses his ability to concentrate, he himself becomes powerless to accomplish, to enjoy, and, above all, to love.

We love that which we give our concentration to, and we concentrate on that which we love. The person who has a passion for skiing will have no difficulty concentrating, practicing, and performing, but the individual who is on the mountain primarily for some other reason—for example, to prove something to himself or others—is more in love with his image than with skiing and is apt to find himself easily distracted.

CHOOSING TO CONCENTRATE

Concentration is a discipline we impose on ourselves for a purpose. We are used to constraining our bodies; for instance, we give up a large measure of physical freedom for five to six hours when we fly from New York to Los Angeles, but in doing so we reach our destination quickly. Likewise, when we choose to concentrate, we sacrifice the freedom of our minds to take excursions into the past or future. When we choose to go skiing in the first place, we are forsaking a book, business, or the Caribbean for the sake of what we hope to experience by skiing. Every act of saying yes to one activity requires saying no to many others. To deliberately make the choice of a particular person or activity is therefore a profound compliment. On the other hand, to be involved only in terms of physical presence is an insult not only to that person or activity but also to yourself.

Once the decision to go skiing has been made and you are standing at the top of the slope, there are still numerous choices. If you want most to improve your form, it might be best to focus attention on your body and listen to its kinesthetic feedback. Increasing concentration in order to overcome fear is another alternative. Or if you are interested in simply having fun and letting yourself go, you may decide to try to abandon all Self 1 control and let your run take you for a ride. There are innumerable choices; all that is important is to make one of them. Otherwise Self 1 will have a hundred ideas for you simultaneously: I've got to perfect this turn before the end of the day . . . I should be practicing my pole plants . . . I wonder if there's anyone to ski with this run . . . I should be concentrating more . . . I should be relaxing more . . . The instructor said I wasn't rolling my knees enough to the inside . . . Maybe I'm thinking too much. Without choosing to concentrate, Self 1 can drive you crazy with inner- and outer-game thoughts, scattering your energy in many directions.

Making the choice to concentrate is to practice disciplining your mind and directing your own awareness. It isn't necessary to stay on a single object of concentration for an entire day, but it *is* a good idea to focus on a single target for a reasonable period—at least until it is no longer producing benefits or retaining your interest. The discipline of sustained focus is an important part of the process of concentration, but extending it is possible only if you don't force it.

For instance, if you decide to try to increase awareness of your edges for two or three runs, and your mind starts thinking about bending your knees or about your ride up in the chair lift or anything else, don't be angry at yourself; simply bring your concentration back gently. Training the mind is like teaching a wild animal; if you punish it for not obeying you, it will turn on you. Firm but gentle persuasion works better. With continued practice the mind increasingly comes under our control. The process is slow and gradual, but constantly rewarding.

Parking the Mind

When a person decides he wants to begin the practice of controlling his mind, what is most important to remember is that true concentration is a relaxed state of mind. Take the example of a skier who after a couple of "bad" runs recognizes that it is his lack of concentration that is keeping him from performing at his best. He decides he must concentrate more and tries to force it, but his skiing only becomes worse and he soon finds himself tense and frustrated. Finally he gives up and says, "The hell with this, I'm just going to have some fun." He takes off down the slope whistling a tune, forgetting all his problems, and has a marvelous run. He concludes that he skis much better when he's not concentrating.

Although many of us have drawn this same conclusion in similar situ-

PRACTICES
IN THE
ART OF
RELAXED
CONCEN-
TRATION

ations, it is not that we ski better when we aren't concentrating but that we concentrate better when we're not trying to. With the song in his head the skier was occupying his striving mind, reducing his tension, and freeing Self 2.

Many people unconsciously tend to sing or hum to themselves to relax their minds and induce a corresponding rhythm in the body. Once in an Inner Skiing class, Carl Wilgus from Sun Valley asked us to sing a song as we took a run. For some reason I chose "Tea for Two," and I skied down the fall line just as if I were dancing to this old melody. At "tea" my skis would turn to one side, and at "two" they would have already shifted to the other. I wasn't thinking about what I was doing; I was skiing as if I had nothing to do with what was happening. It was a wonderful run; I moved better and more gracefully than ever before. When I stopped and watched the others in the class, I felt that I knew the rhythm of the song each was singing by the way they were skiing. Carl, who had "boogied" down the slope, had been singing the Beatles' "Eight Days a Week." Another, who seemed almost in a trance, had been humming "Moon River." Everyone enjoyed the exercise so much that we traded songs and danced the rest of the way down.

This stage of concentration, which could be called "parking the mind to music," is like counting sheep to help us fall asleep. The exercise distracts our mind and lulls it into a rhythm that induces sleep. As the mind relaxes, the anxious thoughts that were keeping us awake or interfering with our skiing disappear.

There are many ways besides music to involve Self 1 harmlessly while simultaneously evoking qualities helpful to our skiing. For instance, imagining yourself as an animal can be both effective and fun. In one class we created a zoo. I chose to be a lion; other students selected a snake, a leopard, a gazelle, an eagle, and even a chipmunk. We came down the moun- tain roaring, hissing, and squeaking, and each person's skiing actually resembled the animal he had chosen. I was aggressive, the snake slithered, the leopard was graceful, the gazelle was elegant, and the eagle floated—but I never could figure out what the chipmunk did.

Many people are under the impression that you have to be serious to focus the mind, but having fun is actually conducive to concentration. When the mind is enjoying itself it is not so easily distracted.

In another exercise I sometimes choose a word conveying a specific quality I want to evoke on my next run. Repeating a word such as "aggressive," "graceful," "easy," or "smooth," my body tends to reflect that quality in its movements. Again, the trick is to absorb Self 1 in the rhythm and meaning of words so that your true potential will be freed. The music or evocative symbol shouldn't be one that requires much conscious effort; the purpose of the exercise is simply to occupy Self 1's attention while the greater part of our awareness automatically attends to our skiing.

Direct Concentration

There are two basic functions of any practice of concentration. One is to decrease the interference of Self 1; the other is to increase our awareness. Parking the mind occupies Self 1, but it doesn't necessarily increase feedback. Both goals can be accomplished simultaneously by focusing on something that *is* happening and is directly pertinent to our skiing. Think of everything that is involved when you ski: body, terrain, sounds, knees, shins, arms, ankles, skis, edges, snow. Anything you can sense, feel, see, or hear when skiing is an appropriate object for concentration.

Foot Concentration

One of the most vital yet most overlooked areas of concentration when you are skiing is your feet. They are connected to your skis and they affect every movement you make. "A good racer's concentration," writes Warren Witherell in *How the Racers Ski*, "is on the feel of his edges in the snow. He can feel the texture of the snow, the shape of the terrain, and he is sensitive to the flex and shape of his skis."

An instructor and racing coach at Sun Valley once told me that he seems to feel every inch of his skis when he is going down a mountain: "It is as if my skis were part of me." In order to develop sensitivity of this sort, it is necessary to heighten the awareness of your feet, to sense each part of them in detail. The next time you ski, focus on the soles of your feet. Feel how the weight is distributed: Is it more on the balls of your feet, the heels, the insides, or the outsides? Notice where your weight is when you traverse, and how the pressure shifts during a turn. To keep your mind involved, call out where this pressure is at different times during a run and rate it on a numbered scale. This kind of detail can keep your mind absorbed, which makes you more sensitive to your body's feedback. One caution: don't become overly concerned about the accuracy of your numbers—call them out quickly without thinking.

After a while, awareness of your feet will extend to your skis and you will be able to feel their flex, the subtle changes in terrain, and the bite of your edges on the snow. Can you imagine how well you could ski if you had the awareness and control of your skis that you have of your feet? Or better yet, if you had the control of your feet and skis that you have of your hands? Think of how subtle and fine your turns would be with this degree of awareness.

Foot awareness can also be practiced off the mountain by noticing how your foot lands and where the most pressure is when walking or running. Many skiers lose this awareness when their boots are too tight or their feet are cold. They curl their feet, which is not only uncomfortable and cuts off feeling, but also causes tension in the ankles, shins, and calves, preventing flexibility and fluidity of movement. Cramped toes make it painful to put our weight forward, and usually cause us to lean back, a dangerous habit that can cause a lot more pain than just in our toes. A good way to experience foot awareness is to try the following exercise. Take your shoes off and place your right foot on a tennis ball. Let the ball roll under your foot, feeling it make firm contact with every part of your foot. Then stand on both feet and note how your right foot feels in comparison with the other. Most people find that it will be more relaxed, more in contact with the floor, and more sensitive.

Skiing Centered

When Self 1 is in control, our attention is usually in our heads. When we think too much, we tend to become top-heavy, as if there were extra weight above our shoulders, and consequently we easily lose balance. But when we move freely and easily in a state of relaxed concentration, our natural center of gravity—the point of perfect balance—is located just below the navel. If you watch great athletes or dancers closely, you will see that their movements seem to originate from this center.

One year I gave a class three technical instructions at once and asked that everyone do his best to follow them. Trying to implement them on the next run made each student think a lot, thus keeping the focus fully centered in his head. The next time we came down the mountain I suggested that everybody shift his attention to his pelvis. Afterward the response from the class was unanimous. When the focus was centered in the mind, the students couldn't feel their feet or skis, and their heads hung forward as if leading their bodies. Everyone felt off balance, awkward, and mechanical. However, when their attention was on their natural center, they reported that they felt more relaxed in the upper part of their bodies and that their skiing felt smooth, flowing, balanced, and effortless. Centering also results in greater stability and gives the skier better contact with the snow, which in turn leads to better control.

An instructor from Lake Eldora recommends that students imagine they are skiing at night with a flashlight in their bellies that shines on the terrain in front of them, showing them where to go. This simple exercise focuses concentration and encourages the initiation of movements from the skier's center of balance rather than from his head or shoulders.

Seeing

Though excellence in skiing is mainly dependent on the quality of kinesthetic feedback, visual feedback is also essential. The eyes act like a scanner, constantly giving us input regarding subtle changes in the pitch of the slope and the texture and depth of the snow. The body will react to what the eyes see as long as Self 1 doesn't screen off this information by making judgments.

One way of increasing visual concentration is to pretend that the ski slope is a giant canvas and that your skis are brushes. Each run you take becomes a stroke on the painting and each turn a curve. Looking down the slope before and while skiing it, you can imagine what kind of stroke would be best on this particular terrain—long, short, smooth, or squiggly. Your eyes then guide your body through your run; you simply let the changes in terrain teach you how to "paint" them. Since we see better when we don't think that we know everything about a trail, it's a good idea when practicing visual concentration to ski it as if for the first time.

The next time you ski, notice how far ahead of the tips of your skis your eyes fall naturally. Many people, concerned with the position of their skis, tend to look at them constantly, and thus don't gain feedback from the slope. Others look too far ahead. Experiment with focusing on different distances until you settle on what works best for you.

Listening to Your Skis

Most skiers will concentrate either on the feelings of their bodies or on seeing the trail; it rarely occurs to them to listen to the sound of their skis. But if you listen closely you can hear distinct variations when the skis are flat or on edge. Even the varying conditions of the snow create different sounds. By involving the additional sense, that of hearing, our minds become even more concentrated, and the feedback we receive increases our control.

One day, while listening to my skis as I practiced, I began carving beautiful turns with virtually no skidding. There was a smooth and muffled sound, as opposed to the *whoosh* of a skid. Resisting the temptation to analyze what I was doing right, I simply asked my body to keep reproducing the sound. It worked; holding the sound in my mind, to my amazement my body kept reproducing it. Occupying Self 1 with the memory of the sound of a carved turn, Self 2 was free to repeat the actions which had produced the sound.

Broad and Narrow Concentration

The choice of what to concentrate on is easy if you want to practice edge control or if your pole plant is so rough that it throws your timing off. That is, you focus on something that is relevant to those difficulties. However, occasionally there is nothing specific that you want to concentrate on; no single problem seems more important than another. At such times simply keep your awareness general; instead of narrowing your field of concentration, broaden it.

If concentration is like a light shining upon a target, general concentration would resemble a broad searchlight. A wide focus on your body will reveal any tension or imbalance that needs particular attention. When such a problem emerges, you can turn your broad searchlight into a more powerful and focused beam to acquire more feedback from that area.

If you focus for too long on one area of your body or your skiing, concentration might become strained, and it is then time to relax and return to a more general awareness. Broaden your light again and become aware of your rhythm or balance as you come down the mountain. Sooner or later something more specific will again emerge. It is perfectly natural for your concentration to veer between the general and the specific as you ski.

Breaking Through Your Mind

In the stages of concentration discussed so far, the mind has been either "parked" or focused, but in the breakthrough stage of concentration your busy, chattering mind stops altogether and you enter into a world that is pure experience. You are calm, quiet, immersed in your activity. There is no separation between action and awareness, thinking and doing. You are in total harmony with yourself and your surroundings, and all else—time, space, past, and future—pales before the present moment. Athletes call this state "playing in the zone."

Fine, says Self 1, but how do you get yourself into this state? Aye, there's the rub; you can't make it happen any more than you can make yourself fall asleep. You can prepare yourself for sleep by lying down on a comfortable bed, closing your eyes, and relaxing your mind, but the final stage can't be forced. Similarly, you can't control the attainment of the state of oneness, but you can prepare for it so that it is more likely to happen. In the final analysis, the breakthrough stage of concentration is a process of letting go, so don't look forward to congratulating yourself if you do achieve it, because the instant you do so you've returned to your thinking mind.

THE MASTER SKILL

Whatever experience we gain in the practice of relaxed concentration helps us understand the theory behind it; conversely, as our understanding of the theoretical aspects develops, our practice improves. Theory without practice won't help us, but the necessary practice won't occur unless we understand the importance of concentration in our lives.

Earlier it was stated that concentration is a voluntary discipline that we impose on our minds for a purpose. If the reader's primary goal is to improve his skiing, then his practice will be only as diligent as the importance he places on the sport. But relaxed concentration, though necessary to excellence in skiing, is also a requisite for any kind of excellence. The very quality of our daily experience depends on the development of this master skill. The quality of our concentration can make the difference between a life that is satisfying and alive and one that is incomplete and dull.

Two skiers can stand atop the same mountain, and one can be experiencing a transcendent beauty while the other is seeing just another mountain. The difference in the quality of their perceptions lies in the quality of their attention. Similarly, you can ski a beautiful run but not really appreciate it, while on another day you can take the same run with less proficiency but, because of the quality of your concentration, really enjoy yourself and learn more from the experience. Skiing well doesn't automatically lead to an experience that is good, nor does skiing poorly have to lead to one that is bad. What makes the difference is the ability of the skier to appreciate whatever happens.

This understanding is really the essence of Inner Skiing. The quality of our enjoyment and the excellence of our performance depend primarily on *internal* conditions. Value lies *within*, not without. A small improvement in our internal ability to perceive can outweigh many external changes because it has the power to change the entire range of one's experience.

Take an example. If you take a home video with a camera that has a scratched lens and a faulty focusing device, what success will you have? The footage shot with such a camera is going to be inferior, but you might mistakenly conclude that it was the locale you chose. Of course, the tape still doesn't come out well, whatever spot you pick, so you may end up complaining that there's no place on earth that will give you the footage you want. However, if the scratches are removed and the focus repaired, it will make all the difference in giving you successful footage of even an ordinary place.

This camera analogy does not fit our human situation in one important way: that is, a camera is not affected by the object it is exposed to, but a human being is. In *The Inner Game of Music*, Barry Green pointed out that a person who enjoys fine music will be uplifted by it, and his ability to appreciate it will be increased by its quality. Likewise, a steady diet of inferior music tends to lower the consciousness of the experience and makes it more difficult, if not impossible, for one to value an especially fine piece of music.

Hence, it is common sense to seek out those experiences that are conducive to uplifting our awareness, not only because the experience itself will be more satisfying, but because it prepares us to better appreciate the next one. What good will it do a man to be in an ideal situation if, because of an uncontrolled mind, he is not aware enough to appreciate it?

My father used to tell me the story of a guard at the Louvre whose job was to protect the *Mona Lisa*. Often tourists would come up with cameras, stare at the painting, and turn to him and say, "What's so beautiful about her?" His reply was always the same: "Monsieur [or madame], it is not this picture that is on trial."

Skiers and nonskiers alike tend to assume that the quality of their experience is the result of what is happening to them, so we put too much energy into changing externals. We look for better ski tips, better jobs, better homes, better husbands or wives. Although we can alter our lives by changing our environment, most significant changes occur when we find effective ways to change our inner landscape, because that is the environment that we will always have with us.

Experiencing is our fundamental activity, and so the quality of our lives depends on the quality of our experience. And the quality of experience depends on state of mind and on depth of concentration. If my life isn't as satisfying as it could be, is this the fault of my circumstances or of my ability to appreciate them? Is the cause of my discontent internal or external? Are not most of our external conflicts a result of our internal unrest? Much of the time we are so caught up in the content of our lives, the "goodness" or "badness" of what happens to us, that we forget to take any joy in the very fact that we are alive and are able to experience life at all. Regardless of the texture of our lives, we are privileged to be participating in the process called living. Whenever I can see my life from this point of view, I begin to free myself of the pettiness of Self 1 concerns, and to appreciate the best my life has to offer. And with what do I appreciate it? With the gift of awareness, with the quality of my attention, and with the power of my concentration.

9❄
LEARNING
TO
SNOWBOARD

O ne day people were skiing down slopes working on parallel turns, balance, and weight control, when suddenly and without warning the slopes that had been more or less the same for years were punctuated with exclamations from a new brand of snow player. They were young, daring, and free, carving wide arcs on a single ski called a snowboard. What went through skiers' minds? What was it *you* thought? Maybe on one occasion the young boarders had come too close or they might even have run into you and you weren't sure it wasn't partially intentional. Or maybe you noticed that most were under twenty-five, spoke a weird language, and were trying stunts that no one in their right mind would attempt. Maybe you were one who hoped they would be banned from the mountain, or maybe you simply decided that snowboarding was not for you.

Yet in spite of early resistance from the more conventionally minded skiers, this new sport gave no signs of going away. In fact it soon became the fastest-growing winter sport. Whatever reasons skiers might have for avoiding this challenge, very few can honestly say that they haven't looked across the self-created chasm between skiers and snowboarders with some degree of admiration of the kind of moves that can be made on a single board. Could it be as much fun as it looks?

This chapter is not about convincing anyone to snowboard who doesn't want to; it's for those who would like to learn to have an easier and safer time of it. The main argument that I will present in favor of considering snowboarding is that it could be a beneficial adventure, inviting the development of valuable learning skills. Everyone realizes that

WHY SHOULD A SKIER LEARN TO SNOW- BOARD?

131

the biggest leaps in learning tend to happen during the first year of a sport. Such breakthroughs are thrilling in comparison to the incremental changes that occur after one is more seasoned. Besides this, there is much to be gained from learning anything from scratch. The terrain will look different, balance will seem different, the moves required to stop or turn will be different. In this sense the sport is, for the skier, an apt metaphor for learning how to cope with change in a world where learning to learn is becoming the most critical skill for success in any field.

In a recent conversation with a championship-level snowboarder, I asked about the most difficult challenge skiers faced in learning the sport. "Their ego," he said without hesitation and as matter-of-factly as if he had said, "Learning to stop." He went on to explain that what seemed the hardest for them was to have the willingness and patience to spend the time needed learning the basics of snowboarding on the "bunny slopes" when they had been skiing easily down the advanced slopes. This is the exact problem I have seen so many executives face when they find themselves forced to change careers due to technological advances or when they are asked to take on totally new responsibilities within the same company. Suddenly they are thrown into a realm where they lack the competencies of a professional. Yet in their minds they are still professionals. So the thing they most need to learn, even more than a new set of competencies, is how to be a learner again. Once a person realizes that he or she can be a professional in one domain and a beginner in another, without undue offense to the ego, that individual is at a great advantage.

The rest of this chapter will focus on how to learn something new using snowboarding as the case in point, but with the hope that you will be able to transfer what you learn to the learning of any new skill.

LEARNING TO LEARN

Learning to learn has been widely acknowledged as the most critical skill for succeeding in the twenty-first century. Knowledge and technology are evolving so rapidly that "what" to learn is becoming increasingly harder to anticipate. But the *how* of learning is timeless in its value. And perhaps of equal importance is the *how* of unlearning. It can be much more difficult for people to let go of long-held ideas and assumptions than it is to learn something new. The skier who takes up snowboarding will have the chance to practice both the learning of new skills and the unlearning of old habits.

One of the most important things I have learned about learning and helping others learn is about vulnerability. The learner is vulnerable. To not recognize this, whether as a learner or a coach, is to ignore a most crucial factor. And why is the learner vulnerable? It's not just because of the potential for physical injury, but because learning takes place on the edge between the known and the unknown. It always has and always will. And the realm of the unknown—where you don't yet know and can't yet do—is a place that makes the most confident person feel vulnerable, vulnerable to looking ignorant and incapable, states not so readily tolerated in our culture. Yet this is the nature of learning and also why many very competent people have difficulty with it.

So the first principle of learning is to make it as safe as possible—not just physically safe, but psychologically safe as well. Above all, you don't want to let a student, or yourself as learner, feel like a fool. Self 1 will now probably take the opportunity to remind you of feelings and thoughts that you may not have had since early school days. The wise coach therefore goes out of the way to create a learning environment that is safe and introduces challenge only to the extent that the established safety allows.

At the beginning of the learning process there should be a high degree of safety and minimum challenge. Psychological safety in the Inner Game approach to learning is achieved by replacing judgments about right and wrong with nonjudgmental observations.

Step 1. Asking Why

WHERE WOULD YOU START IN LEARNING SOMETHING NEW?

Personally, I would start with a basic question: What would be the benefit to me of learning to snowboard? Probably nothing is more important in learning than motivation. It's only to the extent I am clear about *why* I want to learn that I will have the motivation to stay focused and to persevere through the difficult times. I would watch people snowboarding, not to see how they did it, but to see whether it looked like fun to me. When observing different boarders, I would allow myself to "get into their boots" and imagine that I was experiencing whatever they were on the board. Imagination is a great simulator and brings you close to the real experience at no risk. I might also talk to people who snowboard, ask them about what they like about it and about any concerns I might have, such as safety and degree of difficulty. I would stay in this observing mode until the spark of desire was ignited.

Step 2. Playing Around

The next thing I would do is play around with the equipment. I have found this process invaluable at the beginning of any kind of learning. Playing around means not trying to learn anything, just "messing around" without much intention. It's what children do automatically and is part of what makes them such good learners. Playing around serves two functions; first it creates an environment of maximum safety, without expectations or judgment. At the same time, whether you're playing with sports gear or a new idea, you gain a familiarity with the basic equipment. And because that familiarity is gained in a playful atmosphere, the relationship between you and the new equipment you will be using will be a friendly one. This period ends when you have played enough with the variables at hand and are familiar enough with them that you begin to get bored. Even if your Self 1 starts telling you that you're wasting valuable time and not progressing fast enough, don't listen to it. Allow your childlike spirit to spend all the time it needs at this stage of the game; it will shorten and ease all future steps.

My First Excursion

How would I specifically accomplish this step in snowboarding? First, I just walk around the area where the snowboarders are gathering and perhaps watch them put on their equipment, store it, and observe whatever logistical details will help me feel more at home when the time comes to get started. I'm always surprised by how much I can pick up just walking around, listening, and observing, not even knowing what I'm looking for. I ask around about where a good place is to rent equipment. I want to get fitted with a board and boots by someone who knows what they are doing. I decide that I will spend a half day just playing around with the equipment before meeting the instructor who has promised to teach me.

My next step is to look for the safest possible environment in which to play. I want it both physically and psychologically safe enough to be a total beginner without embarrassment. I settle on the grassy area in the backyard of my condo. On the grass I explore not only the physical aspects of the equipment, but start to get used to the feel of standing on the board with both feet strapped in. I can get familiar with what it feels like to edge up on one side of the board and then the other. I find how to move my body to retain balance.

When I no longer feel like a complete novice, I move my play to a flat area where there is snow, but no people. I push the board around like a toy car watching how it moves in the snow. I push it down a gentle slope and watch what it does. I do whatever I find interesting with the board in the snow without strapping in. Then I decide to strap one foot into the bindings and try the same balancing moves I did on the grass. I try skating on the board, pushing off with my free back foot; and with one foot free for balancing, I glide down the gentle slope. I'm learning to balance on a slowly moving board. Then I tip the board back until I fall, then find out how to get up, and then fall forward.

134

After experimenting with one foot for a while, I strap the other in. Skiers who had tried snowboarding had told me that it felt awkward and somewhat claustrophobic to have both feet confined on the same board and that it was hard to regain balance without having two independent skis. I decide I'm not going to try a slope yet, and explore how it feels to have both feet in the bindings in a static position. On a flat area of snow I rock forward and backward and test the limits of my balancing ability. After a while it doesn't feel so awkward.

I'm becoming familiar with the simplest aspects of balancing on a board and feel ready to meet my instructor for my first lesson. I know that the comfort I gained will allow me to put full attention onto learning the core skills of snowboarding. I'm ready for Step 3.

Step 3. Learning the Initial Skills in the Awareness Mode

The next morning I get up early and with just a little anxiety seek out my instructor. I also feel the anticipation of learning something new and know that I have no idea how difficult or easy I'm going to find it. I think again about why I am wanting to learn and try to get mentally ready for whatever is to come my way.

My instructor is Pat McNamara, a fifty-three-year-old competitive snowboarder who tells me with respect that borders on reverence, "I stole everything I'm going to teach you from some of the best snowboarders in the world." He mentions working with champions Brian and Kevin Delaney and then says, "They are all great athletes and have the greatest hearts."

The first thing he teaches me is how to pick out my equipment to make sure it is a safe system and a good fit. He also insists that I wear knee pads and wrist protectors as well as a helmet. Then he asks me an interesting question: "Visualize yourself running toward a large frozen pond. Knowing you want to slide on the ice, which foot would you lead with?" "My right foot," I answer with instinctive certainty.

"Okay, then you are goofy," he replies matter-of-factly, "not regular."

Those were the first words in "snowboard" I'd heard. *Goofy*, he explained, was not a bad way to go, but simply a term describing a way of standing on the board with the right foot forward toward the tip of the ski. "*Regular* is leading with the left."

"Okay. If you say so, I'm goofy."

My board checks out okay, and after about five minutes of stretching exercises he starts joking around and making crazy falls in the snow, inviting me to follow. At the end of ten minutes of childlike play, I do feel more "goofy" than "regular," but my beginner's anxiety is gone. "The snow is your friend, not your enemy," he says, as he takes me to another area.

Much to my surprise, Pat then begins to lead me in a series of exercises similar to those that I'd tried on my own yesterday. We do balancing exercises, walking the board and pushing it with one foot and sliding as if I were skateboarding. I feel familiar with most of the exercises and think that he must think I'm a fast learner. But he says nothing except to ask me to notice things about how my body feels and how the board moves in the snow. The only challenge is to pay attention to what is happening. It feels safe, because there are no instructions about doing it right. Just play. Soon I feel comfortable and ready for the next step. "Can I try going downhill?" I ask with some anticipation.

We walk our boards about twenty yards up a very gentle slope. With tip pointed down the hill, he says, "Just let gravity pull the board down the hill. Follow me." No problem. I'm moving so slowly that balancing is not much more challenging than when skating on the flat snow. "Feel as much as you can about how the board feels on the snow as you are gliding," Pat reminds me.

"You sound just like me, when I tell my beginning tennis student not to worry about getting the ball over the net, but to just 'feel the swing.' I think I've found the right instructor," I tell him.

We continue with one foot gliding down for a half hour, and I become more and more aware and increasingly comfortable and balanced on the board. At the end of this segment of the lesson Pat says, "I can tell you are having a lot of small kinesthetic successes." My body is feeling warmed from inside and a little tired from the use of new muscles.

After a fifteen-minute break, we walk our boards to a rope tow. I watch him as he takes hold of the rope and follow. There's an unexpected jerk as my hands tighten around the slowly moving rope and I momentarily lose balance. I'm glad I still have one foot free and soon I'm being pulled along easily and find a place on the board for my rear foot. It is the first time I experience balancing in motion with both feet on the board. I realize that each step in my learning is so small as to be almost unnoticeable in the physical sense, but is very rich experientially.

Once at the top, Pat helps me strap in my rear foot while sitting down on the snow of a very gradual slope. When I stand up with the board across the slope, he asks me to lean back a little and balance on my "heel side." I can feel my back edge of the board cutting into the snow. "Now flatten the board and see what happens." The board begins to slide. Instinctively I rock back again on my heels and the sliding stops. We repeat this move over and over. Sliding and stopping, sliding and stopping for about fifty yards to the bottom of the hill. It's slow and easy, and gives me beginning confidence that I can maintain balance while sliding and that I can learn to stop. I didn't realize how much these "feels" were going to be the foundation of my future snowboarding experience.

We take the tow back to the top again. He gets me on my hands and knees, board across the hill, and gives me a hand up. Still holding my hands he asks me to put weight on my toes. Now I can feel the front edge digging into the snow. I play around with different degrees of edging, then let the board be flat, feel the sliding, then stop with my front edge. Encouraging me to play around with this edge, I start to slide down the hill and stop, slide and stop just as I had on my back edge. But this time I feel more adventurous and want to see how far forward I can lean without falling. I find out. By falling, of course. Soon I'm searching for my balance point—where "too far" is and what just far enough feels like. Pat is simply leading me in the exploration without instructions. There is a good feeling of independence in the self-discovery process he's allowing. He tells me to explore angling my board up and down, back and forth— all the possibilities—including falling intentionally a few times on both heel side and toe side. Before long I feel confident of my balance on the board in motion and that I can slide or stop on either edge at slow speeds. I can definitely feel the new muscles I am using.

We take another break. Pat explains, "Pushing beyond your limits of fatigue is where you lose attention, and where learning stops and accidents begin. Remember this," he warns firmly.

After the break, he tells me I am ready to learn to traverse the slope. I watch him glide across, moving just fast enough to stay in motion. "I can do that without falling," I think to myself. Pat is more concerned with a different aspect of my safety. "Before traversing a slope, always be sure to look uphill to ensure no traffic coming down." Then the only instruction is "Keep looking at me as you move toward me." I focus my eyes on his as if I'm watching a tennis ball and find myself gliding easily toward him. As I arrive there's a smile of satisfaction on my face. "Did you notice where your weight was balanced on the board?" is his only comment. No, I hadn't noticed. "This time, find out," he says, moving another ten yards in the same direction. Without knowing where my weight should be, I notice that it's balanced toward my heels and my back edge is slightly angled. "That's called heel-side edging," says Pat, smiling. "Now get on your knees and roll the board over, and we'll try the same thing on your other side." After making sure I check the uphill slope for skiers, he asks me again to fix my eyes on his and this time to point my uphill arm at him.

So back and forth I go, first on one side, then on the other, stopping at the end of each traverse, like an autumn leaf falling from a tree. Glide stop, glide stop. I'm having fun, and by the time we've been up and down the hill three times, I'm having the distinct feeling that learning to snowboard is definitely in the realm of the possible for me.

It's time for lunch and for Pat to explain some of the physics of snow-boarding to me. He tells me about its dynamics in motion during turns at faster speeds. "This won't make a lot of sense to you right now," he says. "I'm just sowing seeds. Understanding will click in later when I'm no longer around." He then starts telling me about my next step, learning to turn at the end of a traverse. "Just watch me making a turn in front of you. I will be waiting below. When you traverse to the place where I turned, just turn your head in my direction, balance dead center on your board without leaning back into the hill, and just trust the board to turn," he explained. "As the board begins to point downhill, it will pick up a lit-tle speed, maybe from one to two miles per hour. But since you will be leaning forward, as you look toward me, your side cut will engage the board and will make a toe side turn. No more falling leaf!" At this point I hear Self 1 whispering its doubt in my ear that all this was too compli-cated to remember, and I would probably fall trying it.

By the time we get to the top of the slope, I'm feeling a little nervous for the first time. He has told me that when the board points downhill during the turn, my tendency will be to lean back toward the tail of the board, and that doing so will add even more speed to the board. "This is where most students fall," he cautions. I start feeling anxious, not so much because I'm afraid of falling, but because I don't want Pat to think I'm like "most students." Self 1 is getting a little foothold, but I recognize the voice as not mine. "Hey, what's wrong with being like most students," I retort. I remind myself that I'm not on the snowboard to prove that I will never make a mistake and that if I remain a *student*, the worst that can happen is that I will learn something and that is the also the best thing that can happen.

Note: This was a more important lesson than I realized at the time. Pat told me later that most of the foolish risks that are taken by snowboard-ers are in the name of "proving something to friends" instead of being content to "stay within themselves." I needed to be reminded of this more than once.

As I make my traverse, I'm looking for the spot where Pat had turned. I turn my head toward him and feel the board turn under me and pick up speed. Instinctively I lean backward, feel the board slide out from under me, and I fall into the snow, laughing. I had done exactly what he said not to. This is my first nonintentional fall, and it strikes me as funny. I'm also very glad I have already learned how to get up. Brushing off the snow, I start thinking about what went wrong. Knowing better than to try to compensate for my mistake, I decide simply to focus my attention where my weight is on the board at the moment the tip is pointing downhill. This is another chance to trust in Self 2 and not to try to overcontrol it. Even though I've trusted it a thousand times in tennis, this time feels like

138

the first. And I'm both surprised and delighted when, without trying, I feel my weight more forward as I effortlessly retain balance throughout the turn. My board stops where Pat is waiting, and I have a triumphant smile on my face. Pat seems as delighted as I am. For me there's nothing like the feeling of having my trust in Self 2 confirmed. I never grow tired of the feeling of knowing there's something inside that is worthy of my trust.

Before long I am turning with confidence in either direction. I find how little effort it takes to initiate a turn by simply moving my head in the desired direction. My hips and knees follow my head, producing the turn. I focus on these moves and confidence grows. Pat gives me simple instructions like, "Point your hand toward me, in the direction of your turn." He teaches the hard stuff, but leaves it up to Self 2 to learn from experience.

Now I am linking one turn into another at slow speed. After three runs of linking six or seven turns each run, we pause and Pat says, "Believe it or not, you have learned ninety percent of the skills you will ever need to learn." I realize that this is like telling a beginning tennis player who had just hit a few forehands, backhands, and serves over the net that he has learned 90 percent of tennis. Of course in a very real sense it is true. "What remains is to refine the basic skills you learned and to discover how to do them at higher speeds on more challenging terrain," Pat says. I feel a definite sense of accomplishment even though I have spent the morning on the easiest of the bunny slopes. I'm having fun and know I have laid a good foundation for future learning. Trusting Self 2 is paying off. Just as I am feeling somewhat victorious and ready for the next challenge, Pat says it is time to pack it up for the day.

I don't understand why until the next morning when I awake feeling the sore muscles in my legs. But my eagerness for more snowboarding is also there. I am ready for Step 4.

Step 4. Refining Initial Skills and Practice on More Challenging Terrain

The morning starts with more stretching, rolling in the snow, and more linked turns down the same bunny slope as the day before. Then we walk our boards to a nearby chairlift and Pat shows me how to get on and off. He shows me how to place my free rear foot on the middle of the board between the two bindings, tilt my board up before riding off the chair, and keep my eyes focused down the incline. He gets off first, and it looks easy. I decide not to think about it, but simply "focus on the ball" (Pat's eyes) and trust Self 2. No problem. I ride off the chair and down the incline with pretty good balance. Pat smiles and tells me that nine out of ten people fall the first time off the chairlift. Nice going, Self 2.

The gradient of this slope is slightly greater and we take several more runs just linking turns. On each run, Pat gives me a different focus of attention. One time my knees, the next my shoulders, the next my weight on the board. Always in the background of my mind I am aware of balance. We work hard on braking skills and Pat elaborates on the importance of being aware of the proximity of other skiers and snowboarders who are in the vicinity or might appear from over a rise as if out of nowhere. "In the middle of a hill, you are totally exposed; so if you need to rest, find a place near some trees or next to a sign," he cautions. As we continue with braking skills Pat emphasizes staying within myself, and not allowing myself to go so fast that I couldn't easily stop if I had to.

The Horror of the Hills

"Let me tell you about the horror of the hills," he starts, talking very slowly. I start envisioning some kind of snow-white gorilla coming out of the trees. "Here's what it is. It's when a husband and wife are out on the beginners' slope with their six- and ten-year-old daughters and they both look up the hill at the same time to see two seventeen-year-olds snowboarding straight down the hill at twenty miles per hour, totally out of control. This is what has given snowboarding a bad reputation. They've obviously had no instruction and wouldn't know how to stop if they wanted to. It's like firing a gun into a crowd." He goes on to say there is no need to be paranoid, but there is a need to be realistic and very conscious. "Wear a helmet always," he advises, "even on the easiest slopes. It's just like in a car, you want to have your safety belt on even when stopped in case someone runs into you." I feel sobered.

It is time to learn to refine the basic skills. Pat leads the focus of my attention so that I learn about weighting and unweighting the board and the importance of keeping my shoulders level. I learn how to make a separation at my waist, so I can be dynamic and driving in my lower body while remaining yielding in my upper body, and how to drop down low to the board, developing tension in my quads.

The process of learning each skill remains the same. I watch and listen to Pat and then without trying hard to master any particular new move, I simply give my full attention to the specific part of my body we're working on, and let Self 2 search for the kinesthetic feel that is most comfortable and works the best. Pat gives me an image of the approximate goal to reach and then I use awareness and trust to take steps in the desired direction.

After each series of turns we talk. Before giving me his feedback, he always asks me what I've noticed. He listens carefully for just how conscious I have been during the run. Then if he saw some things I haven't mentioned that need attention, he tells me his observations. He wants me engaged in being aware of every turn and of what is working and what isn't. He doesn't care at all if I make mistakes; in fact, he says there are no mistakes when you are learning, except to lose control. He simply wants me to know as much as possible about what is happening in the moment. That is the discipline. When he points out something that isn't working, he doesn't tell me to correct it, but to make sure I am more aware of whatever move he has indicated. I keep at it until learning has taken root, and then we move to the next refinement. The method of learning is simple and the same at each step. All that changes is *what* I'm learning. This gives me a lot of confidence that I can go as far as I want with the sport.

One of the things Pat emphasizes is the importance of keeping my arms low. "When you ski, you have poles to use for balance, but in snowboarding you have your arms. If you keep them low, you have 180 degrees of movement upward with which to adjust your balance. If your arms are carried higher, you have that much less upward room to use for rebalancing." When I forget about this, I'm glad that he doesn't yell at me to lower my arms. Instead he just shouts the word "Arms." I know to shift my attention to where they are. Sometimes he yells "Arms" when they're in the right place, to make the point that he isn't always trying to correct me, he's just keeping me conscious.

Before long I realize that I need to be in pretty good condition if I am going to continue. I also realize that riding the board could be a thing of real beauty. I'm close to calling it a day. Before we go in, Pat sends me down the hill to watch him come down. "Kneel and look at me. I will come close enough that you can see my eyes—look for where my head and eyes are in relation to my turn. Notice my shoulders. When I'm on the toe side, look at how I drive my knees into the snow. Notice what's happening below my waist. Visualize the suspension system of an automobile." This is a lot to notice, but I know I'm not going to be tested. I decide to just look and let the memory of his words focus my attention.

I feel a little silly kneeling in the snow while two nearby skiers are relaxing nearby propping themselves up with their poles. Pat starts down the hill making beautiful turns on both sides. I see some of the details he mentioned, but mostly I catch the whole picture of the different parts of his body all working in sync with each other. It is poetry in motion. As he approaches me, he has built up a pretty good head of steam. With only a few feet left to stop, he does something that produces a spray of snow, and then a little hop, and comes to an abrupt halt. He's standing erect and comfortably, with his board balanced on a little flat ledge made by his final hop. He has a huge grin on his face. I want to learn to do that, is all I think. I look over at the two skiers standing with mouths open in awe. They say they've never seen anyone stop like that and start to ask Pat how long it takes to learn to snowboard.

Before quitting for the evening, I ask Pat to describe in more detail how he does a heel side turn. Here's what he says:

> I'm coming down the hill on my heel side. When I want to turn, I first look to the left in the direction I want to go. With both arms at my side, I begin to follow my vision across the hill so my upper body rotates and my hips pivot. My knees are driving to the left as I rock my balance back on my heels. The nose of my board snap rolls across the fall line and I am now driving my weight down with my knees and my front edge comes up. My back is straight, and the board is making a smooth arc. The side cut is fully engaged. At the end of my turn, I look to my right, and unweight, causing the board to release and snap to the right from the kinetic energy that has been stored. Now my knees are driving to the right and I have made my toe side turn.

"How much of all that am I doing now?" I ask, without having understood much of what he was saying. "About ninety percent," he says with a smile. "And you still have a lot to learn. But you won't need me; you can now practice on your own till you're ready for the next step."

I realize my lesson is coming to an end and he is putting me on my own. Before I let him go, I ask him about the meaning of a few of the terms I didn't understand, like "snap rolls" and "side cut fully engaged." But for the most part I have kinesthetic memories to match most of the variables I'm going to practice.

The last thing he tells me is, "Keep with the same learning process to refine the skills you have begun to develop. After about ten more days on the slopes, you will be carving heel side and toe side turns down intermediate slopes at twelve to fifteen miles per hour and will be well within your limits of control. And unless I miss my guess, you will be having the time of your life!"

Later, I made a simple table to remind myself of the desired outcomes of a heel side turn and what focus of attention I could use to learn each skill element. Here it is.

Picture of desired outcome	Focus of attention
When I want to turn, I first look to the left in the direction I want to go.	In what direction are my eyes looking? How does this affect my board?
With both arms at my side, I begin to follow my vision across the hill.	Where are my arms? Is my board following my vision?
My upper body rotates and my hips pivot.	Extent of upper body rotation and hip rotation?
My knees are driving to the left, as I rock my balance back on my heels.	Force and direction of knees driving? Center of balance relative to my heels?
The nose of the board snaps across the fall line and I am now driving my weight down with my knees and my front edge comes up.	Snap of the board? Extent of weight on my back edge? Extent my front edge is off the snow?
My back is straight and shoulders level.	Straightness of back? Tilt of shoulders, if any?
The board is making a smooth arc. The side cut is fully engaged.	The arc of the board in the snow? The feel of the edge cutting the snow?
At end of my turn, I look to right.	When do I look back to the right?

Step 5. Selecting New Skills to Learn and Refine (Using Steps 1–4)

It is going to be a while before I am ready for "dynamic suspension system," "advanced weighting and unweighting," and "level shoulders on steeper terrain." But I know that the learning process will be the same and that as long as I stay within my skill level and keep my eyes and ears open for skiers and boarders in my vicinity, this is going to be a most enjoyable adventure.

143

OF FEAR AND FOOLISH- NESS

In some circles, snowboarding has gained a reputation as an "extreme sport," one that can be dangerous in the extreme. Of course, photographs and videos of snowboarders launched into the air, board over head, in the middle of an acrobatic trick looking like Olympic high divers, make very spectacular images. But those committed to learning the advanced freestyle tricks are in a minority, and are doing so in a realm of risk for which I cannot comprehend any equivalent benefit. Obviously Alpine snowboarding has risks equivalent to or arguably greater than skiing. At the time of writing this chapter, snowboarding bindings are not designed to release the boots at the time of a fall. This is an added risk factor. Yet it can also be argued that with both feet on one board, the snowboarder is not subject to the kinds of injuries that result from the skier's legs being pulled in different directions by independent skis. It is prudent to be familiar with the particular risk factors of snowboarding as well as skiing.

Risk, however, does not belong solely to the nature of either sport. It is also a function of the judgment exercised by the individual skier or snowboarder. The most important factor in any sport is managing risk by knowing your abilities and choosing to stay within them.

Chapter 4 distinguished two kinds of fear evoked by two kinds of danger. Self 1 fear is generated by a distorted perception of reality and usually a situation that handicaps one's ability to successfully cope with a given challenge. Self 2 fear, on the other hand, rises from a clear perception of danger and serves the purpose of preparing one for either higher levels of performance or making the choice to avoid the danger. The perception of danger has three separate components: threat, vulnerability, and capability. Threat refers to some set of conditions in the environment that may do one harm. Vulnerability refers to the degree of fragility of one's body, including whatever protection is being worn. The third factor, capability, refers to the ability of the person to deal with the threat at hand. Perhaps I should have included a fourth factor, namely the mental capacity to make an accurate assessment of the first three and make the best decision.

There is no doubt that there are conditions in both skiing and snowboarding that are real and present dangers to any human body, no matter how able. So each of us needs above all to be able to make accurate assessments of the degree of risk involved in any given choice we are confronted with. To the extent one realizes this, one can consciously go about learning intelligent risk management in a way that will be of great benefit on and off the slopes. Life itself is constantly asking us to make assessments of danger relative to our vulnerability and capability. If we mistakenly underestimate either the present threat or our vulnerability or overestimate our capability, we have to endure the consequences. I'm sure everyone has made mistakes in this process in one realm or another, but the point is to learn enough from little mistakes that you won't have to learn the same lesson from catastrophies.

So I would spend plenty of time on the bunny slopes until I had developed the necessary competencies to stay under control negotiating the next levels of difficulty. Here is a good example of where I wouldn't want to learn everything from my own direct experience. I would consult with a more experienced snowboarder who had good judgment and might be more realistic than I regarding my present level of capability and the degree of danger presented by any challenge I might be considering. I suppose it is conceivably more thrilling to succeed at a move that is challenging over a dangerous piece of terrain, and I like thrills as much as the next person. But then there is common sense—the thinking that tells me that the pursuit of thrills that occur by brushing closely with real danger are eventually going to put my body in a condition that will allow for no thrills at all. I don't want to support in myself or anyone else the kind of courage that has gotten so numbed to danger that it takes the extreme peril to "get off." I believe we all like the way we feel when we are totally focused, the times when Self 1 is not bugging us, and we feel heightened awareness. Conditions of speed often serve as a catalyst to focus of attention and therefore to the heightened states of awareness. But there is a difference between enjoying heightened awareness and being an adrenaline junkie. Adrenaline can be addictive and does alter body chemistry. It's a good thing to have around when it's needed. But addiction to it has consequences similar to other addictions—more and more is required for the same results—and sooner or later will result in serious harm to one's body.

I prefer to develop the appreciation of the beauty and freedom of expression that is possible in skiing or snowboarding rather than look for the temporary chemical high that I might get by flirting with danger. Some will say this is merely the wisdom of the elder generation, but not true. I learned it first from a twenty-year-old friend of mine named Hans Rawat who skateboards, surfs, and snowboards with the best of them and was the first to tell me about the importance of knowing your limits and staying within them.

A Note About the Evolution of Snowboarding Technique and Freeboarding

Because snowboarding is such a new sport, it is easier to see how technique evolves. A few years ago there was no book, no technique, and no instructors. There was *only* learning from experience. Now you see the beginning of naming and describing the different moves. Besides *heel side*

and *toe side turns,* there is *sliding* and *spinning, bonking* and *grinding.* There's *spinning frontside* and *spinning backside.* You can learn *wheelies* and *ollies, nollies* and *tail rolls.* Then there are the halfpipe tricks and air time—*frontside air, lien air, slob air,* and *stiffies, backside air, mute air,* and *indy air.* If you want to experience your board over your head, you can learn *handplants, inverts,* and *aerial flips.* You will especially enjoy the *ho-hos.*

Even though there are colorful names for all the tricks, nothing is set in concrete. If you do a trick wrong, you may have invented a whole other trick. Mike Jacoby, the 1991 Overall World Champion, invented what is now called the *J-Tear* during an attempt to learn a handplant. Not knowing how to do it, he went up the frontside wall of the halfpipe, flew upside down and around—180 degrees more than expected, making a *540 backflip handplant.* A friend named it the *Jacoby Tear* and soon it was popularized as the *J-Tear.* Someday there will probably be detailed instructions of exactly how to do the *J-Tear,* and a criteria for assessing every element of form with the rigor of diving judges. But for now the extreme competitions are judged by simple criteria that include aggressiveness, form, fluidity, style, poise, and control, all attributes that can be developed by snowboarders from beginning to advanced levels.

Right now the learning curve for snowboarding is shorter than that for learning to ski. The sport is in a very dynamic phase. If you want to learn, better now than when instruction has gotten too formalized and you're too worried about doing it right to have fun. Furthermore, once the pendulum has had time to swing toward the doctrinaire, you may find it takes a lot longer to learn. Just one warning—my snowboarding coach, Pat McNamara, told me that a high percentage of skiers who he has helped learn snowboarding have never returned to skiing!

AFTERWORD: BEYOND INNER SKIING

Though we have suggested throughout this book that Inner Skiing presents opportunities to improve not only your skiing but also the quality of your life, it should be made clear, before ending, that the benefits of the sport are limited. No matter how much we learn about relaxed concentration or how beautiful our breakthrough experiences, skiing can give us only fleeting glimpses and indirect hints of the breakthroughs we can hope to experience on a more lasting basis. Yet the breakthroughs we do attain on the mountain indicate that there are levels of awareness possible for us that are more beautiful and deeply satisfying than we ordinarily reach in our everyday lives.

But how long can skiing keep one in this wonderful state? Even if we had a breakthrough every time we skied, the moment would always arrive when we'd have to take our final run, pack up our skis, and return to our daily life. What will keep the freshness of our experience from fading into the routine of our usual patterns of thought and behavior? How do we recapture the same clarity of awareness without the exhilaration of skiing to quiet our minds?

Inside all of us is a mountain with no top and no bottom. The skiing there is perfect. The snow is made of pure peace and there is not a trace of Self 1 interference. The chair lift is always available and takes a person as high as he or she wants to go. Skiing this inner mountain has the power to satisfy the human longing to know oneself and the reason for which one was born. This place of perfect peace has always been within us waiting to be sought, but it can be enjoyed only by those who have recognized the limitations of seeking this satisfaction externally.

This mountain is our true self. Skiing it with steady concentration erodes the power of Self 1 to trick us into thinking that we are separate and alone. It leads us to the source of our love and peace. Beyond the barriers of Self 1 it becomes possible to live in a changing world while being aware of that core that does not change.

ABOUT THE AUTHORS

W. TIMOTHY GALLWEY was born in San Francisco in 1938. His international best-seller, *The Inner Game of Tennis*, first published in 1974, put forth principles and methods for learning and coaching that have since been applied to the achievement of excellence in the worlds of business, health, and education as well as in sports.

For the past twenty years, Gallwey has dedicated most of his time to working in the areas of learning, coaching, and peak performance with major corporations and nonprofit organizations. His long-term clients include AT&T, Apple, Coca-Cola, and IBM. His Inner Game work has provided the seminal ideas for more than ten consulting companies that offer services in executive coaching, innovation, and the human side of learning and change management. His findings from his work with these enterprises are expressed in the *Inner Game of Work* (Random House, forthcoming). Mr. Gallwey can be reached at The Inner Game Corporation, P.O. Box 875, Agoura Hills, CA, 91376.

U.S. News and World Report called DR. ROBERT KRIEGEL one of this country's leading authorities in the field of change and human performance. He is a *New York Times* best-selling author, a commentator on National Public Radio's *Marketplace* program, and a commentator for ESPN for the U.S. Professional Ski Team, and he has recently done two specials for PBS.

A former all-American athlete, Kriegel is a pioneer in the field of sports psychology who has coached both Olympic and professional athletes. *The New York Times* said his work "spurred a revolution in performance practices." Dr. Kriegel has taught at Stanford University's Executive Management Program, and he was a member of the California Governor's Council. He is the author of two national best-sellers, *If It Ain't Broke . . . Break It!* and *Sacred Cows Make the Best Burgers.*

ABOUT THE TYPE

This book was set in Berling. Designed in 1951 by Karl Erik Forsberg for the Typefoundry Berlingska Stilgjuteri AB in Lund, Sweden, it was released the same year in foundry type by H. Berthold AG. A classic oldface design, its generous proportions and inclined serifs make it highly legible.